Mastering the 7 Dimensions of Business-Technology Alignment

Mastering the 7 Dimensions of Business-Technology Alignment

Ashish Pachory

BEP BUSINESS EXPERT PRESS

Mastering the 7 Dimensions of Business-Technology Alignment

Copyright © Business Expert Press, LLC, 2020.

Cover Image Credit: Golden Sikorka/shutterstock.com

First published in 2020 by
Business Expert Press, LLC
222 East 46th Street, New York, NY 10017
www.businessexpertpress.com

ISBN-13: 978-1-94999-178-9 (paperback)
ISBN-13: 978-1-94999-179-6 (e-book)

Business Expert Press Information Systems Collection

Collection ISSN: 2156-6577 (print)
Collection ISSN: 2156-6593 (electronic)

Cover and interior design by Exeter Premedia Services Private Ltd., Chennai, India

First edition: 2020

10 9 8 7 6 5 4 3 2 1

Printed in the United States of America.

Abstract

The force-multiplying power of Business-Technology alignment is acknowledged among the biggest contributors to enterprise success in the digital age. Even so, companies that focus solely on a coalition between their business and technology strategies are often crushed in the fierce battle for digital turf, where the big guns routinely clash with start-ups.

Successful digital enterprises define alignment between Business and Technology along *multiple* dimensions. To become successful digital enterprises, they invest in alignment between Business and Technology at the level of their culture, strategy, structure, process, intellect (innovation), function, and tactics. A systematic understanding and embracement of these seven dimensions of BITA is at the core of a successful digital enterprise.

Using familiar workplace paradigms and stories gleaned from decades of experience with global corporations that have shaped the current Business-Technology landscape, this book builds on each dimension of Business-Technology alignment toward strengthening the foundation on which a successful digital enterprise stands, using tricks and tips not found in textbooks and classrooms.

The practical ideas and insights, punctuated by relatable examples, make this book an essential read for everyone who is, or aspires to be, in an organization that relies on a convergence of business and technology to achieve success. It will make you pause and wonder how so much was left to chance on something as critical as integrating technology with business.

This book makes no assumptions of prior skills in technology and business management, and instead builds upon fundamental ideas in a manner designed to strike a chord in everyone—from interns to entrepreneurs.

Keywords

alignment; business–technology alignment; business value of technology; business–it alignment; business–it integration; career; chief information officer; cloud computing; cultural alignment; customer experience management; customer lifecycle management; digital business; digital enterprise; digital mindset; digital technology; digital transformation; digital vision; digital workforce; enterprise mobility; functional alignment; future of work; information technology; innovation; instinctual connect; leadership; outcome-based it; process alignment; smac; strategic alignment; structural alignment; tactical alignment; technology for business; technology management; technology readiness; transformation

Contents

Acknowledgments

One of my hardest decisions yet was to step down from corporate life into the uncharted world of writing, to fulfill an abiding passion. The support and encouragement I received from my family, most notably my mother, Mrs. Madhuri Pachory, and my wife Seema in this difficult transition is invaluable. It is what made this book possible. I therefore dedicate it to them with gratitude and pride.

Behind every story and anecdote in this book are people who lent me their time and insights through interviews and survey responses, patiently bearing with my persistence. Without their support, the narrative would have been incomplete, or at best, obscure. I wish I could name all these people individually and express my deep gratitude but am bound by confidentiality.

This book is but a compilation of the ideas, thoughts, experiences, and stories of the many wonderful people with whom I was privileged to share my long professional journey. Many of the life lessons that make up the essence of this book are drawn from these brilliant folks who will never cease to inspire, and to whom I shall be forever indebted.

Writing a book is not a road on which you travel alone. To all who have walked beside me on this exhilarating path, I can only say this: Thank you for being the wind beneath my wings.

Introduction

The digital economy is the greatest leveler of our times. It is a turf where the big guns battle with startups for supremacy. In this battle, expertise in Business *or* Technology does not guarantee a win, but their alignment does. The force-multiplying power of Business Technology alignment (BITA) has been acknowledged among the biggest contributors to enterprise success in the digital age.

For many organizations, Business–Technology alignment refers to a form of *strategic* coalition only. Often, these organizations rue the fact that business outcomes are not in line with expectations despite their efforts at "aligning." They quickly conclude that BITA is just hype and consign it to empty slogans and platitudes. It is not long before they line up the wayside of the digital racetrack.

At the other end of the spectrum are the digital success stories. These are stories from different industries, sectors, and geographies but with a common thread: They all define alignment between Business and Technology along *multiple* dimensions. To survive as digital enterprises, they say, companies must invest in alignment between Business and Technology at the level of their culture, strategy, structure, process, intellect, function, and tactics (Figure 0.1). A systematic understanding and embracement of these seven dimensions of BITA are thus at the core of a successful digital enterprise.

This book uses familiar workplace paradigms to build on each dimension of Business–Technology alignment toward strengthening the foundation on which a successful digital enterprise stands.

My preceding book, *Aligning Technology with Business for Digital Transformation*,[3] included a BITA calculator, designed to help enterprises measure their alignment scores along each dimension of BITA. This tool is now also available at www.alignedtowin.com While the BITA tool is a useful compass, successfully navigating the ocean of digital business requires an inclusive and *rounded* approach to alignment, which focuses on *every* dimension of BITA.

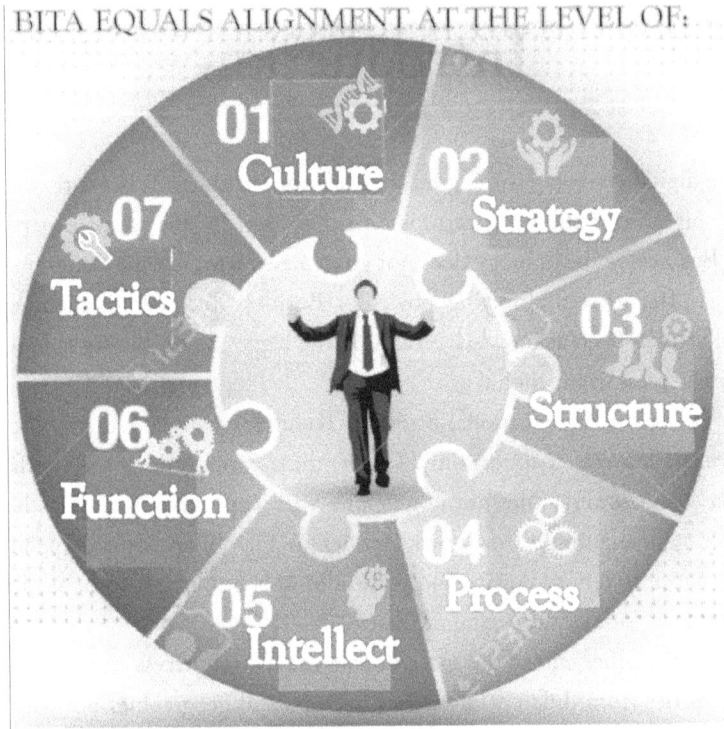

BITA EQUALS ALIGNMENT AT THE LEVEL OF:

01 Culture

02 Strategy

03 Structure

04 Process

05 Intellect

06 Function

07 Tactics

Figure 0.1 The seven dimensions of alignment

The seven dimensions of BITA are the subject of the chapters that follow. Each chapter attempts to (1) help organizations unlock their digital potential and (2) guide individuals in developing the right orientation for succeeding in the digital workplace. The real-life examples, stories, tools, and illustrations make this a practical handbook for harnessing the power of BITA. While browsing *Aligning Technology with Business for Digital Transformation* would be a great stage-setter, it is perfectly possible to read this book independently, without loss of continuity.

The term BITA is introduced in this book to refer to BusIness–Technology alignment. In most organizations, Technology and IT are overlapping functions, so BITA refers equally to Business–*IT* Alignment. In this book, Business with an upper-case B refers to the Business *organization*, while Technology with an upper-case T refers to the Technology (or IT) *organization*. When used with a lower-case b or t, business and technology refer to the respective disciplines, or sphere of activity.

This book is aimed at orientation rather than specialization. In other words, its object is not to teach but to *awaken*. There are two underlying principles it is premised on. One, *everyone*, not just the subject-matter experts, plays a crucial role in influencing business outcomes in the digital economy, and must embrace the principles and practices on which it is founded. Two, it is the *comprehensive*, rather than selective, focus on *all* the seven dimensions of alignment—presented in the following chapters—that leads to a sustained edge in the digital economy.

Whether you are a member of the corporate workforce or aspiring to become one in future, gaining mastery over the seven dimensions of alignment, in measured steps, is the recipe for developing the softer skills and mindset to succeed in the digital world.

CHAPTER 1

The Culture Connection

"We are what we repeatedly do. Excellence then, is not an act, but a habit."
[Will Durant]

Culture connects. Accordingly, people align best when they are connected by a common culture. Therefore, let us begin our conquest of Business–Technology alignment (BITA) with a victory over the culture dimension.

Culture is the foundation on which the collective identity of a group—which could be a community or a corporation—is built. It arises from a set of fundamental beliefs that are consciously, consistently, and collectively demonstrated by members of the group in their thinking and behavior. That is why companies have a *belief system*, which prescribes a code of conduct—for example, putting the customer first, conducting business ethically, displaying personal integrity, setting high standards of quality, treating people with respect—that every employee is expected to emulate in word and spirit. The belief system lays the foundation of the organizational culture. An organization has *character* when it does not compromise on its belief system, irrespective of inducements, compulsions, or consequences.

In a word, culture is the organization's DNA. It gives the organization the personality that it is recognized by. However, it is a dynamic sort of personality, as organizational culture must *adapt* to the changing times, albeit with some immutable aspects. Of course, it requires a conscious, organization wide effort to weave an altered set of common behaviors, but culture change *can* be induced. It is important, though, to know your current bearings and the direction to follow, before embarking on the journey of transformation. We'll devise a simple method in this chapter to help in this effort.

As enterprises transform to digital, it is common to have concerns over the cultural shift required. People ask: I can upgrade my technology infrastructure, but can I also transform my organizational *culture* to suit the needs of a digital enterprise? After all, we are now entering a new arena with largely the same set of people who are used to an entirely different cultural setting at work. The short answer is, you *can*. However, even though we have an innate ability as *individuals* to cross cultural barriers and adapt to new settings, when it comes to transforming *organizational* culture, it's somewhat more daunting and cannot be trivialized.

Example 1.1

I was associated with a company many years ago, where a strong and indomitable code of conduct subordinated every other consideration, including business leverage. The belief system was so strong that at no point was an employee of the company in doubt, or fear, about the course of action to be taken in a situation. Even though the corporation extended to all corners of the country, had diversified interests, and an ever-increasing number of employees, it was able to stitch it all together with a common thread of beliefs. The company made a considerable investment in building a culture around its core beliefs, and it was clear to everyone that if there was one thing bigger than business, it was beliefs. As was to be expected, the corporation acquired an excellent reputation as an open, honest, and trustworthy place that customers felt comfortable doing business with, and employees took pride in working at.

Over the years, the corporation continued to expand into more businesses and geographies. Its reputation almost always preceded it. This company has now transformed into a digital enterprise with serious changes to its culture while retaining its core beliefs. Where earlier, it was a rather conservative company with strict hierarchy and protocol, aversion to risk-taking, clear boundaries, no-frills policies, and a formal atmosphere, it was now a thriving digital enterprise teaming with Millennials, flat and collaborative organization structure, performance-based culture, technology and innovation-driven environment, and a fun place to work. But its core beliefs were unaffected by the metamorphosis.

An energizing culture meticulously kept up over the years packs a punch that is hard to beat as a promoter of your business interests. A few years ago, I was in the United States on a project assignment. One day, our business development manager for the region requested me to accompany him to a prospect in another part of the state to help him with the sales presentation. We met the technical director of this prospective customer, and I was asked to give a quick overview of my experience. When I touched upon my work with this company that I spoke of in the earlier paragraph, the Technical Director's entire demeanor changed. I could see that there was a lot more respect in his eyes. He related a story of his own experience with this company, on how every member of the company's staff was zealous to the point of obsession about the quality of the deliverables. Their team, he said, never missed a deadline, and every team member brimmed with professionalism and courtesy, even while working into the wee hours. It was a bit embarrassing for me, more so as I was accompanying the business development manager of the competitor to that company! But I realized at that time what a powerful force culture was in not only guiding people's behavior but promoting business interests farther than one could imagine.

Organizational culture is like a mighty wave that can lift the enterprise to new heights. The trouble is, it can also plunge the organization to low depths from which it may be unable to surface. Bad culture mostly goes unnoticed by the company's board until it reflects in poor financial performance, and by then it's too late. If you are part of a bad culture, it sticks to you, and you reach a point where you are unable to shake it off, deterring potential customers and employers. It's a vicious quandary from which only the exceptionally talented or the astonishingly fortunate can hope to emerge unscathed. My advice to folks who approach me for career-related guidance is, therefore, always to do as much research as possible into the *culture* of the company and ascertain how closely it resonates with their personal belief systems. If there is a good match, they can be assured of a healthy and long-term association. All else can be learned, but culture must be *blended* into.

Example 1.2

This is an example of a company (let's call it XIT, as we can't name it for reasons which will become obvious in a moment), where unscrupulous business practices were misconstrued as a "results-driven" culture. It is a call for organizations to be more judicious in encouraging behaviors that may become ingrained as culture.

Several years ago, a large paper mill in north India invited bids from IT companies for desktop computers and networking equipment to be installed in their factory and offices, which were on the same premises. It was a large deal in a market that was fiercely competitive and hence had piqued the interest of several companies, out of which three had been short-listed based on the price quotes, including XIT. From this point on, it was a level playing field, and the decision would be based on delivery, quality, and so on, not price. When the XIT team was invited for the discussions with the purchase committee, they opened with the announcement that they had already got the equipment delivered the previous day and it was in the customer's warehouse. This shook the committee quite a bit, as they had issued no purchase orders or instructions to the warehouse to accept incoming material. It was an infringement of their policies. Yet XIT kept flaunting it as an example of exceptional service, saying that they had got their deliveries done in anticipation of the order and of course, in the extreme unlikelihood of their losing the deal, the customer could always return the equipment. Clearly, a method designed to put the ball in the customer's court. XIT had obviously assumed that such a tactic would bind the customer to them because having already crossed the price barrier, what better way to demonstrate fast delivery than one that preceded the Purchase Order (PO)! They failed to realize that they had unduly interfered in the customer's purchasing process, put unwarranted pressure on the committee, and worst of all—as it emerged later—offered inducements to warehouse staff to accept the consignment in the absence of relevant documents. No wonder it created quite a flutter and (possibly) termination of the services of some warehouse staff. One thing that did happen irrevocably was the disqualification of this company from the tender process and its disbarment from tendering in the future.

What is the kind of "bring-the-deal-home-at-all-costs" ethos that would pervade this company, persuading its people to overlook the fact that ethical boundaries had to be transgressed, personal beliefs thwarted, and the customers' policies disregarded to close a deal? Over time, this company that had started quite well a decade ago shrunk to a quarter of its size and eventually got sold off to a foreign competitor and finally vanished from the scene altogether. A lot of its people were out on the market, no doubt many capable ones among them, but couldn't find suitable jobs. The importance of investing effort and time in building a strong cultural base cannot be overemphasized, but many companies have been surprisingly short-sighted on this point and proven to be equally short-lived.

A digital enterprise may be born digital (digital *native*) or turned digital (digital *migrant*). Eventually, natives and migrants must conform to comparable cultural codes, but their journeys may be quite different. Typically, a migrant enterprise would need to cross over from a legacy culture to a digital culture while retaining the *kernel*, or the *core* beliefs. That is, it will have to let go of some contingent practices like deep hierarchies, centralized decision making, resistance to change, aversion to risk-taking, and so on, as it acquires new ones like flat organization, emphasis on outcomes, continuous innovation, and risk-taking. However, the *core* beliefs, which could include ethics and fairness in business dealings, and unrelenting organization wide focus on customer experience, are *not* compromised in migrating to a digital environment.

As an analogy, think of your car's wheel. It consists of the central hub and the tire (UK: tyre) surrounding it. The tire must be changed when it gets unfit for the road, while the hub remains. Migrating to a digital culture is somewhat similar. You retain your core beliefs—like the hub—while you change your peripheral behaviors—like the tire. The trick, of course, is not to confuse the hub beliefs with the tire beliefs, or vice-versa (Figure 1.1).

To be fair, though, bringing about lasting cultural change is a bit more involved than changing a car tire. Cultural change does not result from an instruction manual, or a nicely crafted memo from the CEO, or an articulate speech delivered in the town hall meeting (though these may help). It must be carefully and sensitively injected into the enterprise environment through leadership example, rewards, encouragement, role modeling, and continually focusing and guiding people on the right way. It takes time to seep into every nook and corner of the enterprise. Your *existing* culture can have a strong constraining or liberating effect on

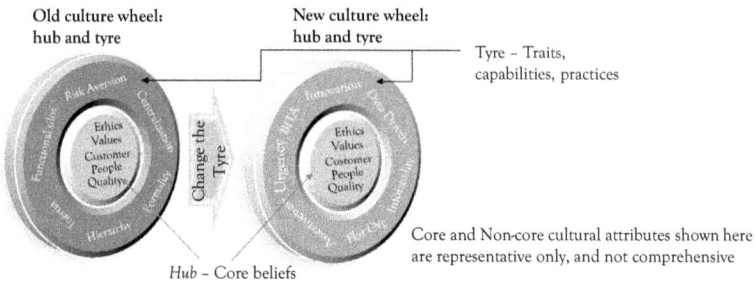

Figure 1.1 Transforming culture

generating the change you need. Build on the preexisting behaviors that support the desired changes and reinforce them continuously.

Culture gives an organization its identity, which in turn determines how the world sees and experiences it. An organization has internal attributes, or its *nature*, and external attributes, or its *persona*. Internal attributes are reflected in the organization's people, processes, priorities, and practices, while the external attributes refer to how it is seen by the outside world, including its customers. In Table 1.1, some differences in culture between an outmoded traditional organization and a new-age, BITA led digital organization are enumerated, taking both internal and external attributes.

The cultural characteristics in Table 1.1 reflect *peripheral* behaviors. The cultural *core*, meanwhile, may remain largely unaltered by digital migration. It is the core that gives the enterprise its grounding. It is *not* situational. This core has probably been the result of years of conscious effort, starting from the founding fathers of the company. Large global conglomerates like IBM, GE, and Tata have cultivated their unique personalities based on the core cultural ethos they have espoused, which they have not given up for digitization. Digital natives like Google, Facebook, and Apple, among others, have also built their inherent personalities as companies that listen to customers, create great products, and have a work environment to die for. Many young and successful digital startups also have deeply embedded cultural cores that set them apart from their peers.

What is this cultural core? Does your company have one? Think about it—what are the three (or more) values or beliefs that have remained unchanged for at least the last seven years (or since your company started)

Table 1.1 Cultural characteristics

SN	Traditional (analog) enterprise	BITA-driven digital enterprise
	Internal Attributes	
1	Layered, slow decision making based on rigid workflows and designated authority	Rapid decision making by an empowered front line with access to relevant systems and data
2	Multilevel hierarchical structure where your behavior is predicated on who is N or S of you	A flat hierarchy where levels don't matter. Abilities do
3	Emphasis on teamwork (i.e., what are we going to do?)	Emphasis on alignment (i.e., who do we intend to become?)
4	Formal relationships, constrained by strict protocol	Informal relationships, liberated by shared ideas
5	Discouragement of risk-taking (openly or covertly)	Encouragement of risk-taking (openly)
6	Emphasis on tasks, methods, processes, policies—you can blame failure on these	Emphasis on the outcome. Innovate, find a way around constraints
7	Technology is a back-end productivity enhancer. Select few understand technology	Technology is a front-end business driver. Being tech-savvy is required for every role
8	Inertia and acceptance of status quo characterize the environment	Continuous innovation and challenging the status quo characterize the environment
9	Age and experience matter. Progress is a function of seniority and gray hair	Only ability and potential matter. Progress is a function of performance and gray cells
10	The organization exists in silos. The only way to communicate across silos is "cc to boss"	Open and transparent organization. Frequent, informal cross-functional interactions
11	Business and IT, at best, work in *agreement* mode on a case-by-case basis	Business and IT are always fully *aligned* and share a common cultural ethos
12	Lack of accountability beyond own functional area ("your problems do not resonate with me")	Shared sense of urgency pervades the organization
	External Attributes	
13	Mindset: "Customers must buy what we have produced."	Mindset: "We must produce what the customers want."
14	Ideas impacting customers and business partners generated internally in isolation	Customers and business partners participate in generating ideas that impact them

15	Focused only on satisfying current needs of stakeholders	Focused equally on anticipating and meeting future demand from stakeholders
16	Supply-driven. Focused on purchasing, manufacturing, distributing	Demand-driven. Focused on fulfillment
17	Service refers to incident management	Service means customer experience management over the entire lifecycle

---

Exercise: *Looking at both sides of Table 1.1 as a primer, tag the characteristics that most closely reflect the culture in your own company. What do you conclude? Are you leaning toward an analog or a digital culture? For each of the analog characteristics marked by you, recommend the top three actions you would take to move from analog to digital culture.*

---

and that you are sure will *not* be compromised in the future as well? If you cannot answer this question off-hand, look at Table 1.2 and tick off at least three values on which your company would *never* compromise, irrespective of the consequences. Easy enough? What about you as an individual? What are the values that would prompt you to jump ship if compromised?

This is a random list of some attributes that form the cultural core. See if you can add to this from your own experience in your present or past organizations. Do these guide your behavior even when not in the boss's line of sight?

Table 1.2 Core beliefs

Integrity	Transparency	Accountability	Diversity
Customer-centricity	Respect for people, trust	Ethical conduct	Commitment to learning
Emphasis on Quality	Emphasis on service	Emphasis on safety	One company
Intolerance for mediocrity	Fairness (impartiality)	Environmental sustainability	Openness to change

Example 1.3

Xanonymous Informatics (not the real name) started about three years ago in Pune, India, as a value-added partner of a European IT security corporation under an exclusive agreement for the development of advanced security solutions for the global finance industry. It was the only program they ran, but with a niche domain and exclusive contract, things looked good for this company, and it scaled up quickly to about 60 highly skilled people at the end of one year and about 100 in 18 months, with a 100 percent utilization rate. When the company had started, the founders had clearly articulated a vision for the company to guide it for the next three years. The company also stood out from most startups as one that had a robust and openly verbalized belief system that emphasized respect for people. In a sudden development, the European principal was acquired by a Japanese software firm, which already had a development center in India. As Xanonymous Informatics had not yet generated demand from other companies in Europe, United States, or Asia, it had no choice but to retrench most people at short notice. Unfortunately, the matter was handled quite insensitively. Affected employees were dismayed one morning to discover that their access cards had been disabled, and pink-slips *were insensitively handed out to them by security strongmen at the reception area. No discussions. This was completely out of line with its belief that stressed respect for people, leading to several unpleasant episodes with the departing employees. A lot of these employees claimed that its culture was only a façade and even called the company inhuman.*

The question is, can business exigencies subordinate the belief system or its practice? Business pressures can undoubtedly call for difficult measures, but it is at such times that the culture is put to its real test. Businesses can, and often do, turn around, but if you let go of your beliefs, you lose your character, and that certainly is a lot tougher to rebuild.

A lot can be construed about a company's culture (and character) from the way it treats (a) job seekers and (b) job leavers. How does this work in your company?

Culture does not lend itself to any standard formulas to give it a fillip, or to any form of metrics for measurement. It is intrinsic to the organization's spirit. However, given its role in shaping the enterprise, culture requires assessment too. And this must be done by the body most central to its existence—the people of the organization.

A method to ascertain the cultural footing of your organization is introduced below. This will help to identify areas that need improvement as well as nurturing.

This is a simple exercise which has no preconditions except that it asks you to come in with an open mind. In general, organizations respond better to such exercises in a *workshop* mode, facilitated by a neutral (external) agency. However, a person elected as moderator from within the group can also do the job.

Remember, perceptions rule when it comes to culture. If it is not *perceived* to be part of your values or behaviors, it is *not* happening. Intents and claims do not matter. So please go with your natural response during this exercise.

Step 1.   Form a group of people who are able and willing to participate in this exercise. The ideal group size is 8–10 comprising a balanced mix of Business and Technology. It may take up to three hours of their time. Communicate the brief purpose of the session at least three days in advance.

Step 2.   On the appointed day, meet in a relatively quiet setting. The room should have a whiteboard, a flipchart stand with about 20 charts, markers, writing pads for each participant, a laptop, and an overhead projector.

Step 3.   The person appointed to be the *moderator* will take the whiteboard and write down: "What constitutes good culture?"

Step 4.   Give the group about 10–15 minutes to individually jot down as many ideas as possible on what, in *their opinion*, constitutes good culture. It is important to remember that this is *independent of the culture in your company*. After about 15 minutes, the moderator may display Table 1.4 for additional ideas to pick from, *if needed* (Ideally, it should not be needed).

Step 5.   When everyone has finished, the moderator goes to the flipchart and asks for inputs around the table. Each person contributes their ideas in his or her turn, and the moderator writes down all the *unique* points on the flipcharts. She does not give "expert comments" on the inputs. After all inputs are taken, there are *at least 40–50 unique ideas* on the Desired Attributes List ("DAL")

Step 6.   It's time for a 15-minute break. But not for the moderator. During the break, the moderator quickly types out the inputs from DAL in a Word or Excel file, which can be displayed from the OHP.

Step 7.   After the break, the moderator displays the Table 1.3.1 on the screen. The aim is to fill up its three columns from the DAL to ascertain how the *value system* of the company is understood by its people.

Table 1.3.1 Values

Definitely not stated or implied in our values	Not sure if implied in our values	Definitely stated or implied in our values
Column 1	Column 2	Column 3

The term *values* is used to collectively describe the organization's *stated* values, belief system, rules, and code of conduct that are meant to guide the behavior of the people in the organization.

Step 8.   Before going further, the moderator explains to the group the meaning of each column of *Values* table so that everyone is on the same page, as described in Table 1.3.2. The group may debate and add/modify the rules.

Step 9.   Each item in the DAL is called out by the moderator and is then placed in one of the columns in Table 1.3.1, as per group consensus. On some points, there may be

Table 1.3.2 Values

Definitely not stated or implied in our values	Not sure if implied in our values	Definitely stated or implied in our values
Finds no mention in the stated belief system	*Articulated only in customer meetings and induction programs*	*Guide to behavior. Stressed in the company code of conduct*
Management hardly ever brings this up in their communication	*Posters, screensavers, company website proclaim it, but not stressed by management*	*Reiterated in team meetings and internal sessions*
Not shared in employee orientation and other programs	*Known cases of the belief and its opposite being stated/ exhibited*	*Never questioned*
No examples set for reinforcing the belief	*Often questioned as no one is sure*	*Included in induction and orientation programs*
	Articulated only during good times	*Role modeling by management*
		Pervades the spirit of the organization

a debate on the column to be used (most commonly in attributes like accountability and empowerment, which could be position dependent). In my experience, if there are even two dissenters, that value is not ingrained, and the attribute should be listed in column 1 or at best 2. Do not attempt to be too democratic.

Step 10.   The moderator populates the Table 1.3.1 as above in real-time until the entire DAL is exhausted. At the end of this session, you have a fair view of the company's values as perceived by employees. It's usually quite insightful to look at the three columns, as an indicator of what people do recognize as values and what is *desired*, but missing or ambiguous.

Step 11.   Having a value system is rather meaningless if it is not *practiced* across the organization in a demonstrable way. The moderator now takes the group's attention back to the DAL. This time she asks for the group's view on the *practice* in the organization concerning each desired attribute.

Table 1.3.3 Practices

Never (or very rarely) practiced	Sometimes practiced (situational)	Always practiced (Never or rarely compromised)
Column-1	*Column-2*	*Column-3*

Step 12. The moderator now displays the Table 1.3.3 on the screen.

Step 13. The moderator explains to the group the meaning of each column of *Practices* table so that everyone is on the same page, as described in Table 1.3.4. The group may debate and add/modify the rules.

Step 14. Taking the items from the DAL one by one, the moderator invites the group's view on the correct column of the *Practice* table to place them in. The Practice table is about "Walking the Talk."

Table 1.3.4 Practices

Never (or very rarely) practiced	Sometimes practiced (situational)	Always practiced (Never or rarely compromised)
Breach is tolerated without consequences	*Practiced only in specific situations (e.g., in good times)*	*Leads to recognition and rewards*
No time, budget, resources invested for implementing	*Cases of consequential action for default are rare*	*Guides behavior in crisis periods*
No role models	*No recognition for demonstrating the practice*	*Role-modeling by management—led by example*
Not linked to employees' personal effectiveness goals	*Belief is proclaimed but no budget/resources given*	*Resources readily allocated for reinforcement*
		Practiced even when no one is looking
		Overrides business priorities

Step 15.   This completes the Values and Practices tables. The workshop ends here, but not the work of the moderator (think before nominating yourself to be a moderator—it is hard work!)

Step 16.   At the end of the workshop, when the workshop participants have gone back to their calling, the moderator prints out the Values and Practices tables that were laboriously created during the day. The next phase is analysis. Though the exercise has probably been insightful, you still don't have much to take back to your management.

The moderator creates another Excel sheet in which he makes four lists, under which he enters the attributes from Tables 1.3.1 (Values) and 1.3.3 (Practices) as follows. Once an attribute is entered in a list, it is struck off from the tables.

List 1: Attributes that are found to be strong in both Values and Practice (common points in column 3 from Tables 1.3.1 and 1.3.3).

List 2: Attributes that are found to be strong (i.e., in column 3) in the Values table (1.3.1), but weak (i.e., in columns 1 or 2) in the Practice table (1.3.3)

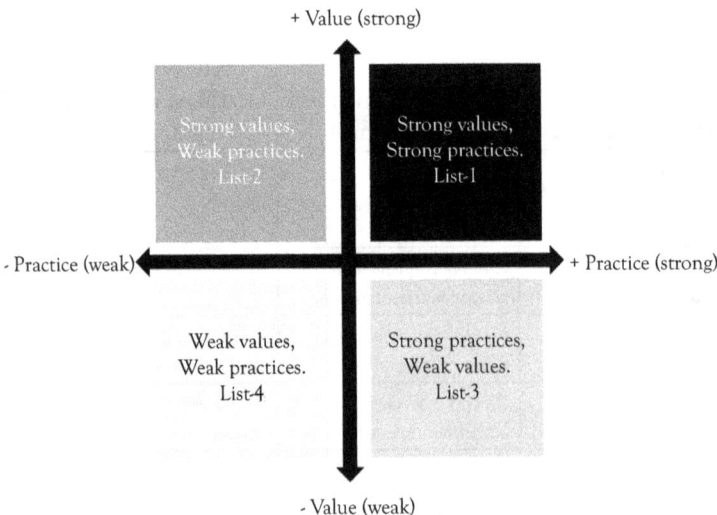

Figure 1.2 Culture dashboard

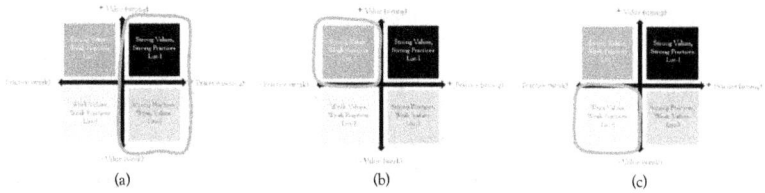

(a)   (b)   (c)

Figure 1.3 Interpreting the culture dashboard

List 3: Attributes that are found to be weak (i.e., in column 1 or 2) in the Values table (1.3.1), but strong (i.e., in column-3) in the Practice table (1.3.3)

List 4: Attributes that are found to be weak (i.e., in column 1 or 2) in Tables 1.3.1 and 1.3.3, that is, both Values and Practices.

Having created the four lists above, the moderator now proceeds to create the *Culture dashboard* as shown in Figure 1.2, listing the relevant attributes in the appropriate quadrants: An automated excel version of the tool may be downloaded from the site www.alignedtowin.com. This would greatly simplify the work of the moderator.

The moderator shares the culture dashboard with the group members on the following day (while the matter is still fresh in mind) and seeks their concurrence. In the event of any strong differences, it may be best to have another quick meeting to reach concurrence.

The attributes listed on the right of the *y*-axis are your cultural strengths, some of which (in the top right quadrant) are ingrained in the value system while some (in the bottom right quadrant) are the good and desirable practices that prevail despite (not being articulated in) the value system (see Figure 1.3a). It is usual for every organization to have good practices beyond the stated values. Good behavior and cultural traits do stem from the embedded value system, and these are non-negotiable, but organizational maturity lies in demonstrating best practices *even* when they are not explicitly articulated in the value system. The bottom right quadrant is, therefore, an indicator of the maturity of your organization. In summary, all the attributes on the right of the axis are your strengths, and these must be preserved over time. Nurture them, most importantly, by avoiding complacency.

In as much as the bottom-right quadrant discussed above is an indicator of organizational maturity, the top-left quadrant (Figure 1.3b) may be said to be an indicator of the degree of *immaturity* in the organization. Let's remember, this quadrant is from the list of attributes that in the collective view of people who participated in the culture dashboarding exercise are the most *desirable* ones for the organization to have. On top of this, all the attributes in this quadrant are included in the prescribed *value system* of the organization. Yet there is no evidence, or even perception, of their inculcation in the organizational *practices*. If you have a long list here, it is indeed unfortunate, pointing to lax attitude and *absence of culture*. Immediate steps must be initiated to dive deeper into the root causes and put in place serious measures to implement and monitor corrections.

The bottom-left quadrant lists the desirable attributes that neither find a place in the articulated value system nor the organizational practices. It calls for more detailed impact analysis to ascertain if these missing traits are the reason behind the organization's failure to retain talent and win the trust of customers and partners. This is a longer-term exercise that may require a detailed internal assessment. Unless it is an unduly long list or has traits that are *significant* in some critical context, put this on the slow and steady. In my view, focus on the top-left quadrant is of much more immediate concern.

Here is a quick summary of the process for ready reference:

1. Create a *Desired Attributes List* ("DAL") based on participants' inputs and Table 1.4.
2. Populate the *Values* table from DAL, per defined rules.
3. Populate the *Practice* table from DAL, per defined rules.
4. Create *Culture Dashboard* by placing inputs from 2 and 3 in the relevant quadrants.
5. Analyze the Culture Dashboard.
6. Identify improvement areas and action plans.

Behaviors take time to weave themselves into the cultural fabric of the organization. Don't expect quick fixes to work here. Ordinarily, the pattern of the culture dashboard will be slow to change, despite concerted efforts to bring this about. The next run of the culture dashboarding exercise should be done at least a year later, with a mix of old and new participants.

After the final concurrence of the group members, present the culture dashboard to your top management and seek their approval on the action plan for improving your culture. In most cases, your astute senior management would be already cognizant of the pattern you are presenting. However, they may be missing the details so go in with proper preparation, particularly on recommendations and the precise support, including the budget for training and other items, that you seek from them.

Based on my own experiences and interactions with high BITA companies, I have prepared a master list of cultural attributes that may provide some pointers during the brainstorming session to construct your culture dashboard. Of course, given the myriad manifestations of culture, there are far too many variations to have a comprehensive list, so this should be taken only as a *sample* list of exhibited cultural features collated from several companies with high BITA levels. As a time-saver, you may conduct the culture workshop with this list in the backdrop.

While no universal "must-have" list of cultural attributes is practicable, you may consultatively draw from the culture dashboard a list of qualities that must be *nurtured* (right of the y-axis) as well those that must be *built* (left of the y-axis), the former being the low-hanging fruit.

New-age digital enterprises are characterized by a sharper focus on technology and innovation, strong Business–Technology alignment, customer experience enhancement, among others. However, some *core cultural values* are still as relevant in the new age as they were in the past. The maturity of the enterprise lies in retaining these attributes even in their haste to garner a greater share of their market, as companies have discovered both to their joy and peril.

Sample List of Cultural Attributes from Some High-BITA Enterprises

1–24 = Entrenched since inception (Hub, or core)
25–70 = Developed/Changed with time (Tire, or peripheral)

At first glance, *all* the cultural attributes are a must-have in the company's set of required behavioral practices. However, it is not practicable to evolve a code of conduct that encompasses *everything*. In fact, this may become counterproductive since no one will be quite clear on what

Table 1.4 Attributes of good culture

#	Attribute
1	High standard of *honesty* and *integrity* in conduct
2	Across-the-board *customer centricity*
3	Uncompromising *ethical business conduct*
4	Passionate about the *vision*, driven from the top
5	Well-articulated *belief system*
6	Business and Technology are 2-in-a-box (high on *BITA*)
7	*Respect* for the individual (not position)
8	*Impartiality* (fairness, lack of bias)
9	*Diversity* (gender, age, ethnicity)
10	No compromise on *quality*
11	No compromise on *service*
12	No compromise on *security* and *safety*
13	Continuous *learning* and *development*
14	Intolerance for sexual harassment (*POSH*)
15	Intolerance for mediocrity (*excellence*)
16	All employees see themselves as "*customer satisfiers*"
17	In-built culture of *reliability* (in commitments, offerings/, dealings)
18	Demonstration of *empathy* (mutual understanding)
19	Awareness and demonstration of *social responsibility*
20	Respect for time—*punctuality* and *discipline*
21	*Achievement-oriented* culture
22	Displaying *common courtesy* toward people regardless of role or function
23	Displaying *sensitivity* to the situation of others–new joiners, interviewees, vendors
24	An atmosphere of mutual *trust* and *credibility*
25	Drive for *innovation*
26	*Go-getter* attitude—find a *way*, not a policy to hide behind
27	*Transparency* and *Openness* (e.g., open door policy)
28	*Flexibility* (willingness to change)
29	*Simplicity* in work processes
30	*One company*—no silos, functional boundaries
31	*Accountability* for results, outcomes
32	*Agile* organization, quick to adapt
33	*Technologically charged* environment (BYOD, Mobility, etc.)
34	Shared *sense of urgency*
35	*Freedom* to express disagreement

36	*Pride* of belonging
37	Information sharing—open and frequent *communication*
38	Strong *alignment* across functions, particularly Business and Technology
39	Emphasis on strong *relationship building* with customers and partners
40	Emphasis on *loyalty*, not just meeting needs
41	*Customer-oriented* frontline (*empowered* to serve)
42	*Minimal supervision*, that is, no micromanagement
43	Appetite for *risk-taking* (dare-to-try spirit)
44	Emphasis on regular *soft skills* (behavioral) development
45	*Value-driven*, not cost-driven, in decision making
46	Taking direct feedback to *include customer views* in design and creation
47	*Solution-driven*, not product-driven
48	Promote *collaboration*—both internal and external
49	Emphasis on building and nurturing *strategic alliances*
50	*New ideas* and *initiative-taking* is encouraged
51	*Sharing* and *cooperation*—generating options, solutions *together* (inter-functional)
52	Keeping customers *looped-in* always
53	Keeping colleagues from other departments *plugged-in* on developments, priorities
54	*Data-driven* and *fact-based* conclusions drive decisions
55	*Listening* to the voice of employees, customers
56	*Value information* (hard or soft) as a critical business asset
57	Focus on impact to business rather than RoI, uptime, and so on (*outcome-based IT*)
58	*Responsive*, not reactive
59	Spirit of *out-doing the competition*
60	*Functional integration*—absence of organizational silos
61	*Lack of fear* in taking customer problems to management
62	Encouragement of *questioning* the rationale behind decisions, policies, processes
63	The *devil-is-in-the-details* approach; getting to the root cause to eliminate problems
64	*Fun at the workplace*—attractive environment for millennials
65	Focus on the *long term*—anticipating the future
66	Reliance on *digital channels* for customer reach out
67	Adoption of Social, Mobility, Analytics, and Cloud (SMAC) for business
68	Making it *easy to get things done* due to the absence of bureaucratic culture
69	Focus on *employee engagement* to boost productivity, motivation
70	A *global* mindset

specifically needs to be focused! It is therefore perfectly normal to have a *few* values and practices that define your personality, but it does not preclude good behavior on the other attributes.

Culture is a unique organizational characteristic that pervades its length and breadth. Everything we have talked about in this chapter applies equally well to Business and Technology together as a subset of the larger organization. A *common cultural root* becoming the foundation for both Business and Technology ensures parity in values, behaviors, and actions, and hence is a potent ingredient for alignment. Without alignment at the cultural level, that is, having a similar stance on the *values* and *practices* that guide behavior, it would be a waste of effort to attempt to reach alignment on the other dimensions. When you perform the culture dashboarding exercise, you define a desired and viable set of values and practices that both Business and Technology agree are the required foundation for achieving success together. Sustaining a high-performing culture, or ensuring the solidity and strength of this foundation, must remain a continuous endeavor of Business and Technology, never to be taken for granted.

It's always easier to exemplify than explain, so let me give a real-life example here on how culture gaps can erode customer loyalty.

Example 1.4

One of the customers of a thriving large digital enterprise in the high-tech solutions business was a medium-sized aspiring digital enterprise with about 60 employees. This customer served a sizeable client base with their merchandising business, centered on sourcing and home delivery of groceries. Things were initially going well between the company and this customer. At one point, this customer approached the company for a lightweight customer relationship management (CRM) system to be used not only for better service to clients, but also to build, over time, a repository of invaluable information on user preferences, buying patterns, and sentiments.

The area business manager mailed the IT team to propose a suitable solution. In due course, with Business and IT working together, a cloud-based CRM solution was devised and proposed. The customer was all for it, as being of a digital disposition, he preferred the cloud over bulky on-premise servers. So far, so good.

The business manager conveyed the customer's expected timeline for the project, which the entrusted IT architect was obliged to sign-off. When the requirements were analyzed, it emerged that there were several parts of the project, like customizing the user interface of the third-party CRM product and performing back-end integration with the customer's existing IT infrastructure, on which the IT team had dependencies outside their control, putting the schedule at risk. Also, the core product (CRM) had to be sourced from a vendor with whom the company had not yet renewed the reseller agreement. The IT architect was taken to task and asked to replan. While all this was happening, both IT and Business assumed it to be the others' responsibility to inform the customer! Anyhow, the teams kept at it on a best-effort basis, but most issues remained outstanding.

When the customer was eventually informed that there would be a sizeable delay, he was quite shaken. His business was a relatively small one, and it depended heavily on this project. The business team meanwhile was more concerned about their year-end quotas and were busy chasing other customers. The matter was left to IT. In a discussion between the customer and IT, the customer suggested a phased approach with a simpler version for the initial launch, but this was not accepted as it would have entailed unplanned effort, which the customer was unwilling to pay for. The customer wrote a harsh letter to the president of the business unit, seeking intervention. A team of technical specialists, accompanied by the area business manager, was rushed to the site for a firsthand assessment of the situation. The specialists concluded that no alternative solutions were feasible from a cost perspective, so either the timeline or some essential features would have to be sacrificed. By now the customer was apparently of the view that if any sacrifice were to be made, it would be of his current vendor! He calmly informed them that rather than reignite the project with a company that had betrayed him, he would cast his net afresh to find another company to work with. Our company had been too complacent to believe that even an existing (satisfied) customer had the option to go to the competition. They lost this customer for good.

Such experiences may sound familiar to many of us. Not because we lack the proper intent, but because we find ourselves at a loss to cope with multiple, and conflicting, demands and priorities. And that is where culture can be your savior. In the above story, at least the following cultural attributes from Table 1.4 were overlooked, to varying extents:

- *Across the board customer centricity*
- *Business and IT are two-in-a-box*
- *Transparency and openness*
- *Flexibility (openness to change)*
- *Shared sense of urgency*
- *Inbuilt culture of reliability (of commitment)*
- *Emphasis on loyalty, not just meeting needs*
- *Go-getter attitude—find a way*
- *Value-driven, not cost-driven, in decision making*
- *Emphasis on strong relationship-building with customers and partners*
- *Feedback loop involving customers*
- *Emphasis on strategic alliances*
- *Spirit of outdoing the competition*

It is quite clear that these cultural gaps were neither recognized nor acknowledged in the company, which prided itself on its strong cultural bonding across its functional units! Some lessons in life are reserved to be learned only the hard way!

A strong culture stems from a set of beliefs and behaviors that are so intrinsic to the core that one doesn't even think of it as culture. That is, culture is that *invisible* force, which compels you to do the right thing in ambivalent situations. It is thus important to assess your cultural footing—using methods like the culture dashboard—before turning to the other BITA dimensions.

CHAPTER 2

The Strategy Statement

"Building a visionary company requires one percent vision and ninety-nine percent alignment." [Jim Collins]

In the olden days, the term strategy was chiefly used in the context of military and warfare. It was a plan of execution centered around one goal: To *defeat* the enemy. At the time, strategy was broadly a two-step process: first, an assessment of the relative strengths and vulnerabilities, and second, a plan to exploit them to vanquish the enemy. The battle maneuvers and tactics stemmed from the strategy.

History is brimming with accounts of triumphs that resulted not from greater strength in numbers or superior weaponry, but better strategy. The battle of Thermopylae fought around 500 BC is the story of a minuscule number of Greek warriors, equipped only with spears and shields, holding off a massive Persian attack—according to some scholars one of the largest armies in the history of medieval warfare—through the courageous attitude of its warriors and a sound strategy. This strategy required, among other things, positioning the troops on the mouth of the Pass of Thermopylae, which was on the only known path through which the massive Persian army could pass to invade. It worked. They could hold off the attack for a full week before being annihilated due to betrayal by a defector who revealed to the Persians another path, allowing them to attack the Greeks from behind. Of special note here is the courage and bravado of the 300 Spartans, distinguished warriors of the Greek army, who defiantly fought the Persians to their very last. The movie '300' is a very engrossing, if somewhat graphic, account of this ancient battle, immortalizing the Spartan warriors.

The above story has a striking similarity to today's world of digital business. The marketplace is the new battleground. Companies, small and big, are faced with the challenge of overcoming very fierce competition.

In such a scenario, the attitude of its frontline Business and Technology people and their alignment to a common purpose are the company's lifeline. Along its way, the company also needs to be on its guard against disruptive forces bent upon its downfall. In the above story, the greatest emphasis was on strategically deploying fearless troops to take on a very formidable enemy. This process evidently started much before the battle, with drafting individuals who could become, eventually, Spartan warriors. Similarly, in the context of digital business, picking people with the right business *and* technology orientation, a never-say-die attitude, and the ability to work interdependently is vital to the success of the strategy.

A strategy is not a directive. An important part of evolving a successful strategy is to ensure that people who are responsible for executing it have a say in formulating it. Top-down strategies are passé. Regrettably, in many companies, a lot of people in the low and middle order go about their daily jobs without having a clue of how they fit into the big picture. If you ask them to state the goal or purpose of what they are doing, they look confused and go into a deep reflective stance, trying to *remember* their purpose! Day after grueling day, they just "turn the wheel," content with being mindless instruction-followers. Taking an analogy from Covey's 7-Habits,[1] they see themselves as aimless stone-crushers, rather than as members of a team building a cathedral! It is difficult to imagine any strategy succeeding in this backdrop, especially in this Digital Age.

The strategy is not meant just for the CEO and the Board, but to provide direction to everyone in the enterprise, particularly the frontline people who are working with customers. It must also consider the interdependence between all functions in the enterprise (see Figure 2.1). If your strategy is not inclusive and interdependent, it is not a strategy at all, but a pretense doomed to failure from the very start.

It is crucial, therefore, to have representation from *each* function in the development of the *enterprise* strategy to ensure buy-in. Once the broader organizational strategy has been *collaboratively* decided at the group level, each function-head must assure its dissemination and acceptance in their team and derive the *functional* objectives from it. This too must be a collaborative exercise. In larger enterprises, this process may have to be percolated iteratively, until each member of every team is clear about the objectives for their team and its correlation with the higher-level enterprise strategy.

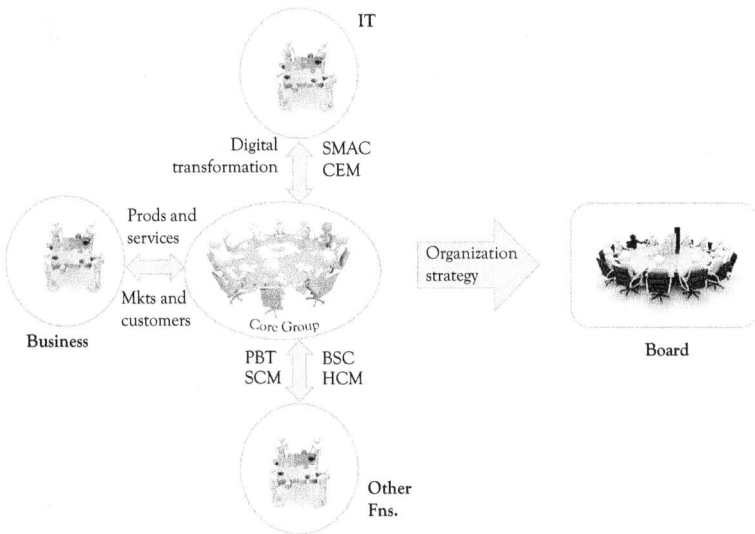

IT

Digital   SMAC
transformation   CEM

Prods and
services

Organization
strategy

Mkts and
customers
Core Group

Business

PBT   BSC
SCM   HCM

Board

Other
Fns.

1. A good strategy has inputs and buy-in of all its stakeholders, not just the core group.
2. Functional objectives must CONVERGE into the unified organizational strategy.

Figure 2.1 Convergence of functional strategies

Convergence is the key to a sound strategy. That is, the objectives of every function must converge into the overall organizational strategy. Functional objectives which are not convergent with the enterprise strategy are untenable and meaningless. They are only an internal plan of action to get around functional bottlenecks that are of no concern to anyone outside the immediate group of people tasked with accomplishing them. It's also against the outcome-based model of IT, with a focus only on input parameters rather than the business/customer-facing output parameters.

Example 2.1

As CIO of a large technology company, I was often asked what the IT strategy of my company was. My answer was always the same, and it was quite uncomplicated: IT exists to make the business successful. Therefore, the IT strategy is simply a plan to achieve the business goals. Everyone in the IT team—even the newest recruits—was tuned to this fact. Every single element in the IT strategy and Key Result Area (KRA) of each person in the IT team had to answer "Yes" to the question: "Does this contribute in a measurable way to making the business successful?" If a person was not clear on how a KRA or strategy statement was accomplishing this, he or she was encouraged to discuss with me and during the discussion, I would either explain the rationale or work with the person and their manager to redraft the KRA. But in no event would I accept a lack of clarity on the strategy or goals. Across the different vertical arms of IT, including the external partners, this simple practice helped to align all teams to a common purpose.

A strategy is derived from the *mission* of the company. However, a mission is typically rather sweeping in its articulation and cannot be readily translated into a strategy. For example, the business mission could be *to help our customers stay ahead by providing lasting value through outstanding software products and services.* How do you accomplish such a mission? You break it down into achievable aims. For example, understand the market pulse, develop new products (to a timeline), improve quality, enhance customer experience, establish competitive pricing while ensuring profitability, and so on. Each of these is a *strategic goal* toward accomplishing the larger mission. The mission is also the basis of the company's long-term aspiration, or the *vision* of its future. There are several such terms commonly used in the context of strategy, which are defined in Table 2.1 for quick and easy reference.

Strategic alignment refers to convergence at *all* stages of the strategy, from mission to KPIs (see Figure 2.2).

Strategic alignment does *not* mean that Business and Technology have the same objectives and action-plans and go about doing the very same things. That would only create a murky blend of uncertain charter. However, it does mean that Business and IT draw their objectives, KRAs, action plans, and KPIs from the same strategic goals. The IT objectives *complement* the Business objectives towards achieving the strategy.

Mission Alignment: As a first important step toward creating a meaningful strategy, and strategic alignment, it is important to assure that the organization is serious about its mission, articulates it clearly, and ensures its dissemination across its length and breadth.

Let's take the case of a company that provides wireless and terrestrial communication services to retail (i.e., personal) and enterprise (i.e.,

THE STRATEGY STATEMENT 27

Table 2.1 *Strategy glossary*

Vision	An aspiration of what the company would like to become in *future*, for example, to be the most admired company in terms of customer value creation.
Mission	The statement of *purpose* that defines the company's reason for existence, for example, to make a positive difference in people's lives through timely, reliable, and secure IT solutions for the Banking, Financial Services and Insurance (BFSI) sector.
Strategic Goals	The mission broken down into a set of *aims*, or intended actions—like enhance customer experience, achieve growth in revenues, conduct business profitably, and so on.
Objectives	The strategic goals supplemented with *measurable* parameters like timelines and targets. Like, achieve revenue growth of 15% over last fiscal by end of year.
KRAs	The specific, measurable, attainable, relevant, and time-bound (SMART) objectives assigned to *individuals* in the group in conformance with the objectives of the *function*.
Action Plan	The set of specific *actions* for achieving an objective. Must have an owner, timeline, and measurement criteria
Key Performance Indicators (KPI)	*Metric* to indicate measure of success against each objective, like schedule variance, lead-to-sale conversion rate
Strategy	The *roadmap* for getting from where you are to where you want to be. That is, a blueprint to guide you in the accomplishment of your mission.

corporate) customers. Let's call this company Aligned Communications Ltd. (ACL). ACL has an extensive cellular and fiber network in its country and is known for its wide range of digital telecommunication services. Of late, it has tied up with services companies (in software, mobility, cloud spaces) to become a next-generation *service* provider and move out of the label of being a utility company.

An example of a mission for ACL could be as below. ACL has invested time and effort in ensuring that this mission is clear to all its employees and partners and that they can relate to it:

Our mission is to create lasting shareholder value by offering a superior experience to our customers across a wide range of communication services using state-of-the-art technologies. As a preferred service provider, we will be a great place to work and a responsible member of our community.

Strategic Alignment

Why do we exist?	**Mission**	At **Company** level
Who do we want to be?	**Vision**	At **Company** level
What must we achieve?	**Strategic Goals**	At **Company** level
What are our measurable targets as a team?	**Objectives**	Specific to **Function** or **Team**
What are my individual result areas and action plans?	**KRAs, Action Plans**	For each **individual**
How do we measure success?	**Measurement (KPIs)**	At every level

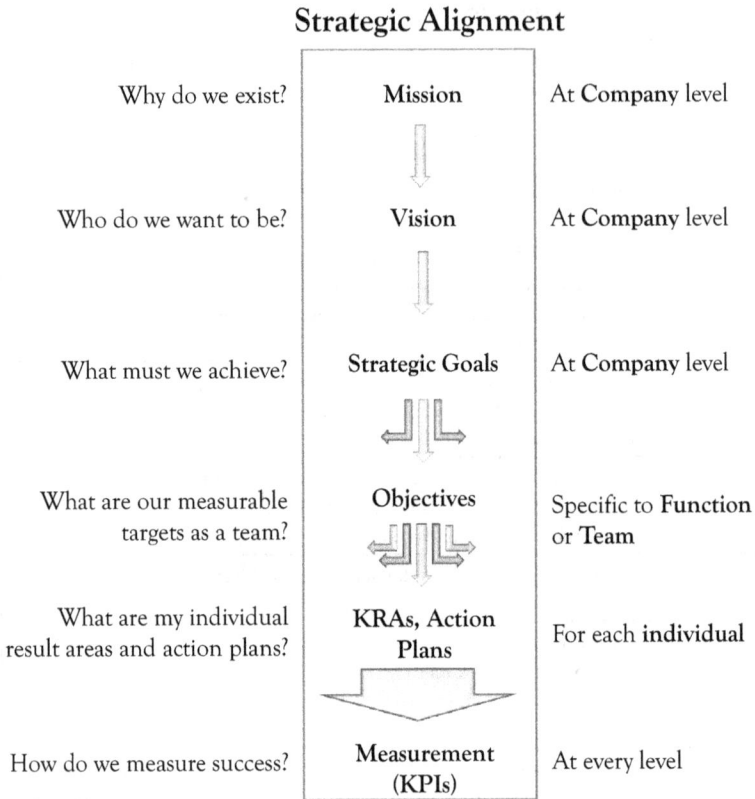

Figure 2.2 Strategic alignment—mission to KPIs

A mission statement is an articulation of the reason for the company's existence. If your mission is not reflecting the organization's real purpose or is not clearly understood by its people, you've lost the race even before you have begun! The mission is the seed from which the strategic goals of the enterprise are drawn, which, in turn, are the basis of the objectives and KRAs for Business, Technology, and other enterprise functions. The mission, therefore, is the foundation for strategic alignment.

Vision Alignment: When you have a clear mission that states your purpose, do you really need a vision for the company? Well, yes. The purpose of the vision is to *inspire*. It reflects your potential for making an impact on a larger stage. Like the prophetic Microsoft vision in the 1990s:

"A computer at every desk running Microsoft software," or the inspiring Intel vision: "This decade we will create and extend computing technology to connect and enrich the life of every person on Earth."

Like mission, the vision must be shared across the company. Different functions or groups within the company cannot be guided by divergent views of the future of the company. That is, for strategic alignment, both Business and Technology are inspired by a *single* vision.

Returning to ACL, let's say its vision is *to be a trend-setter in the evolution of a smarter planet by enabling affordable, secure, and reliable connectivity for the next 10 billion devices.*

This vision, as we see, is independent of function, role, or level, as a vision should be. It applies to, and is an inspiration for, everyone working directly or indirectly with the company. For Business and Technology to align at a strategic level, they must share, and be inspired by, the same vision of the future.

The vision guides the company on the technologies to embrace in the future. While not every new technology can help you grow, and those that can are not guaranteed to succeed, it makes sound sense to assess the implications of new technology on the company and its customers *keeping the vision as the backdrop*. While one strives to stay in lockstep with emerging technologies, it is the vision which guides their adoption.

Goal Alignment: Before the digital era, strategic goals were often different for various functions in the organization. This often resulted in non-convergent objectives across functions and individuals, creating a climate that was not favorable for alignment. It is now increasingly common to define strategic goals at an enterprise level, shared by all functions. That is, *every function derives its objectives from the same set of strategic goals.*

It is customary to segment the strategic goals and objectives along a universal set of *perspectives* that are common to each function. A typical set of perspectives are fiscal, client, external (market), internal (process), and development (human capital) (Table 2.2). The strategic goals are classified under these shared perspectives to facilitate alignment. Here is an example of a set of strategic goals for our company, ACL, along five chosen perspectives.

Table 2.2 Strategic perspectives (Business/Enterprise)

Perspective	Strategic goal
Fiscal	Increase revenues from new products, customers (acquisition)
	Reduce churn levels of high net-worth individual (HNI) customers
	Optimize operating costs
	Achieve profit before tax (PBT) growth
Client	Improve customer experience at all touch points
	Increase customer participation in product innovation
	Segment customer base for differentiated and personalized experience
External (Market)	Sustain brand advantage. Strengthen brand in Eastern India
	Reinforce the network of sales and distribution channels
Internal (Process)	Align Technology architecture with business roadmap
	Integrate supply chain management (SCM), Rev Assurance, Asset Monitoring and Control into ERP system
	Consolidate information management across functions (Company MIS)
	Streamline compliance and governance
Development	Assess and strengthen Business–Technology alignment (BITA) (competitive advantage)
	Implement an effective KM system (empowerment)
	Institute rewards and recognition for innovative endeavors (culture)

The above system of classifying goals is a fallout of the *Balanced Score Card* (BSC)[2] method, which stresses that enterprises also focus on goals other than financial for their all-round and sustained development. This helps in clustering related goals together and enables sharper focus. Both Business and Technology formulate their goals from similar perspectives.

Example 2.2

A company that I worked with as a consultant prided itself on its heavy emphasis on Business–IT alignment. Their CEO informed me that his IT managers carried an objective with up to 20 percent weight "to align with Business." Apparently, that's not how it works. BITA means aligning at the level of strategy, that is both Business and IT drawing **all** *their objectives from a shared strategy, rather than a single "align with Business" goal. And*

> *it must be carried by every employee in the team, not just the managers.*
> *In other words, alignment is embedded in the strategy. It took us several*
> *workshop sessions to finally get to the right set of IT strategic goals. And*
> *real alignment.*

Objectives Alignment: Strategic goals are a great way to set you in the right direction. But to ensure that you don't just keep drifting aimlessly, you need a bearing on how far, or where, you must go (a target) and how soon you must get there (a timeline). That is, to achieve specific results, you aim for tangible outcomes that you can measure and monitor. You need more *objectivity*. A goal that is supplemented with a clear and measurable end-result and timeline becomes an *objective*.

Let us consider the first strategic goal under the fiscal perspective— *Increase revenues from new products, customers (acquisition)*. Business may draw its objectives from this goal as (1) Achieve year-on-year revenue growth of 15 percent, and (2) Increase share of revenue from new products and customers to 12.5 percent. IT may not carry exactly the same objectives as Business but may draw the following objectives from the same strategic goal: (1) Achieve time-to-market on new products and freedom from customer-incidents with 95 percent success-rate, and (2) Increase capacity utilization of existing systems by 25 percent to support new customers without incurring extra costs or performance-loss. If the strategic goal is not met, *both* Business and IT share the responsibility. Similarly, *every* objective of IT must be traceable to the strategic goals from which business derives its objectives, for perfect alignment. If you go back again to the above table of strategic goals, you will be able to formulate correlated Business and IT objectives from every strategic goal. Try to do this as an exercise now.

BITA requires that for each strategic goal, Business and Technology have *complementary* objectives, as in Figure 2.3. Thus, if a strategic goal has two objectives under Business and two under IT, together the four objectives lead to its achievement. They *reinforce* each other. The objectives are defined first at the *function* level, from which they can be progressively broken down into regional and territory level, as well as into product categories and specific product level, depending on how you are organized.

Perspective	Strategic Goal	Weight	Business Objective Goal	Target	Timeline	IT Objective Goal	Target	Timeline
Fiscal	Increase Revenues over the previous year	5%	Achieve Y-o-Y revenue growth	15%	EOY	Timely & defect-free delivery	95%	As per TTM
			Share of revenue from new customers, products	12.5%	EOY	Higher capacity in IT sys with nil perf loss	25%	End of Q1
	Reduce Churn levels. Prioritize HNI base	10%	Retain Start-of-Year base of HNI customers	95%	EOY	Segment and tag HNI customers. Reduce incidents	50%	Ongoing
			Retain S-o-Y base of non-HNI customers	85%	EOY	Reduce cycletime for prepaid charging & incidents	20%	End of Q2
	Optimize Operating costs / Achieve PBT growth	10%	Reduce Opex (over prev year). Subcontracting	15%	EOY	Reduce Opex (over prev year) Outsourcing	15%	EOY
			Increase in PBT Y-o-Y	20%	EOY	Optimize Y-o-Y capex DC to Cloud migration	20%	EOY
Client	Exp-erience at all touch points	10%	Cycletime improvement thru customer lifecycle	25%	EOY	Measured Improvement in cust exp at FA&B stages*	25%	EOY
	participation in product innovation	5%	Set up product innovation lab with dev & test fcility	0	End of Q1	Set up product innovation lab with dev & test fcility	0~	End of Q1
	Segment customer base for differential experience	5%	Establish rules for segmentation	0	End of Q1	Implement rules for segmentation	0	End of Q2
			Personalized campaigns offers per segment	30%	End of Q2	Use of Big data & adv analytics for campaigns offers	50%	End of Q1
External (Market)	Sustain Brand Advantage. Strengthen brand in East	5%	Develop & implement brand promotion plan	0	Ongoing	Benchmark IT with #1 Participate in industry fora	#1 or #2	EOY
	Reinforce network of sales & distribution channels	5%	Strengthen cross-country channel nw per S&D plan	90%	EOY	Design & build channel mgt sys for partner access	As per specs	End of Q2
			Equip co. reps with Mobile soln for channel support	95%	End of Q1	Extend Tablet based access for mobile salesforce	As per specs	End of Q1
Internal (Process)	Architecture w/ Business roadmap	10%	Develop & share 3 year business roadmap	Accuracy Clarity	End of Q1	Modular standard & scalable IT architecture	Busi RM Alignmnt	EOY
	Improve key internal processes (SCM, RA etc)	5%	Optimize critical processes for max impact	10%	Ongoing	Integrate process optimization in Change Mngmnt	TCO	EOY
	Consolidated information management across lns.	5%	Define Business critical dashboards for MIS	Output	End of Q1	Implement tools & sys for data capture & reporting	Timeline Accuracy	EOY
	Streamline compliance & governance	5%	Regular Business-IT reviews and follow-up	Frequncy Quality	Ongoing	Regular Business-IT reviews and action closure	Frequncy Quality	Ongoing
Develop-ment	Assess and strengthen BITA	10%	BITA Assessment (tool based) & improvement	10% overall	Bi-annually	BITA Assessment (tool based) & improvement	10% overall	Bi-annually
	Implement effective KM system	5%	Promote re-use (technical proposals contracts etc)	20%	Ongoing	Cloud based info repository. Re-use (code, solns etc)	20%	Ongoing
	Rewards & Recognition for innovation	5%	Institute spot and annual awards for 'dare-to-try'	10	Ongoing	Institute spot and annual awards for 'dare-to-try'	10	Ongoing

Figure 2.3 Complementary business and IT objectives

KRA Alignment: KRAs are not too different from objectives, except that we refer to objectives in the *team* or *functional* context, whereas KRAs are referred to in the *individual* context. Typically, a team objective is at a relatively high level—for example, achieve revenues of $38 million in the current fiscal, whereas a KRA would be a smaller derivative of this objective. As an individual in the sales team, my derived target may be to "achieve revenues of $2.5 million in the current fiscal" from my assigned territory or product group. Likewise, other members of the team may have their targets such that they all sum up to at least the company target of $38 million. Similarly, other objectives are divided among individuals and sub teams in a distinct but synergistic fashion.

For a good BITA, Business and Technology team members in a *smaller* group—which may correspond to a geographical territory, or customer segment (say, small and medium enterprises [SME]), or product class (say Wi-Fi, for our company ACL)—would have KRAs that overlap more liberally. Smaller teams typically demonstrate stronger cohesiveness.

Building alignment in small groups is therefore particularly crucial because without this, aligning at an enterprise level would be a lot more challenging. It's also *simpler* to build alignment in smaller groups.

Strategic alignment between Business and Technology is not a matter of choice. If required, incentives like linking bonuses to common outcomes may be used, though it may not substitute an inborn exhilaration of being on a winning expedition together.

KPI Alignment: The principle of KPI alignment is based on a simple but powerful premise: If you are *measuring* the same things, you are *managing* the very same things. This is a natural fallout of *outcome-based IT,*[3] a critical prerequisite for BITA. Business has no concern about (or patience with) IT's internal matters. These are *hygiene,* and it is *expected* of IT to quietly find ways around them, instead of making them an issue for the entire organization to be concerned with.

However, most IT organizations are still obsessed with internal measurement and controls, instead of focusing on issues that have a more direct impact on the business outcome. For sure, it is required to track the first-call effectiveness of the service engineer as this, in turn, affects productivity. But this must be an internal matter of IT. I have found that Technology teams that are preoccupied with broadcasting internal trivia almost always fail to prioritize business concerns and lag in alignment.

A village situated between a river and a tropical forest received a warning of imminent floods that would wipe off their homes and belongings. The villagers decided to leave en masse for safer pastures beyond the thick forest. Before embarking on the journey, the village council met and hastily put together a plan to facilitate the crossing. Two teams, let's call them Alpha and Gamma, were created. Team Alpha (in the lead) was tasked with route planning and cutting the thick and prickly foliage, while Gamma cleared the way of branches, stones, and so on. for the village folks, cattle, wagons, and so on, to move. Now, as they moved ahead, Alpha signaled to Gamma on the critical indicators, like how much distance had already been covered by Alpha, the rate of progress so far, the remaining distance to be covered, quality of terrain, and anticipated bottlenecks ahead. These inputs were very useful to Gamma in their own planning of resources

> *and effort, and the progress was generally smooth. But what if Alpha had instead reported to Gamma about the skills and tools it took to cut some branches, the number of times their machetes had to be sharpened, what percentage of branches were cut in one swing of the blade, vs. multiple swings? This would be of no use to anyone outside Alpha and would have hindered rather than facilitated progress. It is the same with IT passionately reporting KPIs that do not matter to the Business, and in the end, they too hinder the accomplishment of the joint mission.*

KPIs are important. They are the mirror in which the company's performance is reflected, based on which future actions and course corrections are planned. Without KPIs, your employees, management, and other stakeholders would be clueless about developments and therefore powerless to act. Hence KPIs must be carefully designed based on the key priorities of the organization. Often, functions report what is *possible* to measure. It must work in reverse. Define what you want to measure and monitor, then *make* it possible to report it.

The simple test of a KPI's efficacy is to ask yourself the question: Why? If you get an answer that directly meets a *business* objective, go ahead. Else, table it for your *internal functional* measurement, but not for business reporting.

The enterprise strategy in the digital era is *business*-led and is the basis of all functional strategies. The enterprise strategy for this reason is sometimes also referred as business strategy, but this is only a label. Functions (like IT) or sub-functions (like Sales) can have their own strategic plans derived from the enterprise strategy, which may become the basis of their functional objectives. But functions or sub-functions cannot become the main drivers of enterprise strategy. A business-led strategy at the enterprise level is the surest route to taking advantage of market opportunities in the world of digital business.

To conclude, the enterprise mission, vision and strategic goals are *common* elements in the strategies of Business and IT. The Business and IT strategies further include their *respective* sub-functional objectives, KRAs, action plans, and KPIs. In a BITA-driven enterprise, the complete strategies of Business and IT complement each other toward the achievement of enterprise goals.

Technology as Thought Leader to the Enterprise

What is the role of Technology in matters of piloting and steering the enterprise? How would a company like our ACL plan for new standards like 5G, or technologies like Internet-of-Things (IoT)? Well, in a Business-aligned organization, Technology is also an influencer[2] of the business strategy and is instrumental in keeping the business tuned to future technology trends that have potential for enhancing business competitiveness. Strategic decisions on their induction are thus arrived at collaboratively, which also leads to increased ownership. There is, however, no justification for investing in future technology that is *not* weaved into the enterprise strategy by common consent. This highlights the role of Technology as a *thought leader* in the organization. A technology roadmap that is insulated from the enterprise or business strategy is an open invitation to failure.

In companies that differentiate themselves on the merits of their technological prowess, sometimes the technology strategy may begin to dominate the enterprise strategy. Some influence of the technical strength of the company in its overall strategy is healthy, but not dominance. Finally, it is the customer who, through the Business function, sets the course, and Technology must adjust its sails accordingly. Yet, there are frequent instances of Technology functions becoming all-powerful and endeavoring to *lead* the Business, especially in product-led services companies and software consulting firms.

Example 2.3

This is the story of a company with a mixed reputation—no one doubted the technological superiority of its products, but its standing as an implementer of customized solutions around them left much to be desired. The technology (project) team and the business team here were separate islands. What prevailed here was a "handover" system and not collaboration. The only alignment that existed was short-lived bursts of enforced cooperation.

Due to conflicting priorities, projects were often delayed, sometimes suspended midway due to sudden, unilateral diversion of resources. Customers were incurring additional costs due to the uncertainties.

Due to the long implementation project cycles and lifetime support requirements, the Technology team was pivotal to the customer's experience. This led the Technology team to believe that they were calling all the shots. They openly blamed Business for making unrealistic commitments without their consent! Arrogance clouded the vision of delivery teams. They wanted a bigger say in business decisions and planning. It was just a matter of time before the strategy of the company was dominated not by market and customer expectations, but by delivery limitations (and whims). In many accounts, business account managers lost their grip on their customers.

Meanwhile, customers were sensing the brewing trouble. In the case of one large client, when the delivery team felt that the customer was "locked-in" as he was over the point of no return, they suddenly diverted vital project personnel to another project. The customer was so incensed by this that he suspended the project and ousted this company.

This customer happened to be among the company's largest global accounts, with whom the company had been entrenched for a decade. Competition moved in on this opportunity. The reputation of the company started falling as customers shared their experiences among each other.

Matters reached such a point that the company had to seriously restructure itself, including several changes at the top management. While Technology was still the backbone of the company, it was not allowed to undermine the business role, and from a "horizontal" function, it was made into a demand-assigned "vertical" under the business account. Customer advocates were nominated who championed the customer internally. Many meetings were scheduled between the company's top management and the customers to apprise the customers of its efforts. The company is yet to regain its former glory in many markets but is now a lot more business-driven and open to listening to customers, surprisingly even small customers in emerging markets. At the time of going to press, the company is in the process of reinventing itself as a BITA-driven company, a concept that it would have scoffed at some years ago.

At the core of a business-aligned Technology strategy is the cycle of interdependence.[3] This cycle begins and ends with the business strategy, as depicted in Figure 2.4.

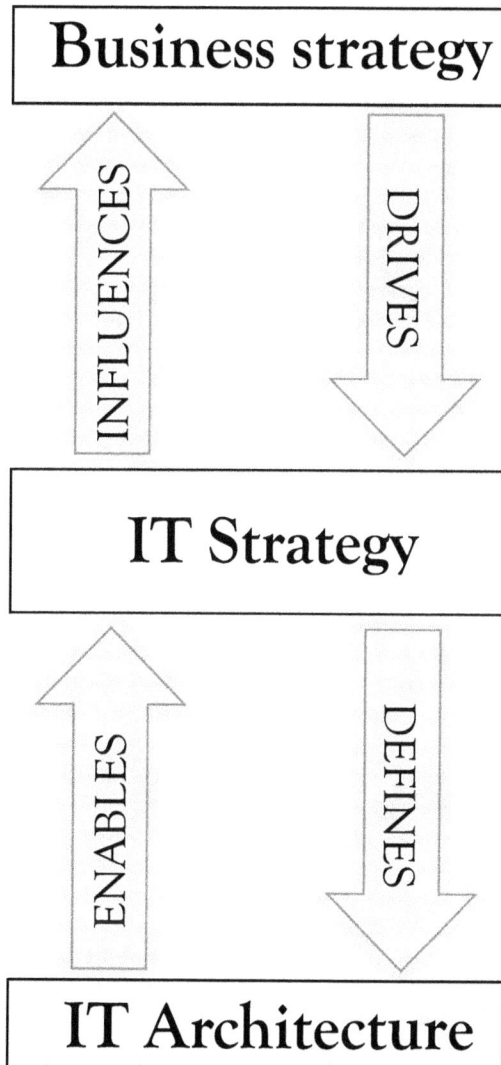

Figure 2.4 Strategic interdependence

Let us close with an important reminder. One may have a sound business strategy or a sound technology strategy, but if they are operating in isolation, no value is created. For real business value to be created, the business and technology strategies (along with key functional strategies) must be aligned and work in unison. In other words, the business and technology strategies are the powerhouses that form part of the same circuit for the creation of business value.

CHAPTER 3

The Structure Story

"An organization is nothing more than the collective capacity of its people to create value."

In a survey at a leading banking and financial services corporation, respondents were asked to identify the biggest problem that they faced in dealing with the Technology department. Options included competency, business awareness, prioritization, future readiness, and sense of urgency. The result? *None of the Above (NOTA)*. Surprisingly, what came out on top was "finding and getting to the right person" in the Technology function. While the extent may vary, this is a common gripe across companies. In my interactions with Business folks from various organizations, I learned that most people were vaguely aware of the function head's name and perhaps a few others, like the helpdesk guy who showed up to fix problems, but Technology as a function was a black box to them. When I met the related Technology folks, they showed surprise that their organization was not as transparent to the Business folks as it was to themselves—no rocket science here, they said, maybe Business didn't try hard enough!

This has some severe implications for BITA. If Business views Technology as a formless entity ensconced behind a dark and mysterious door that has no handles or hooks, there is no place for Business–Technology alignment even to exist. In such a scenario, Technology as a driver of business success is a total misnomer. At best, it is a weak apologist for office productivity extender.

What makes this situation appalling is the laid-back attitude of both Business and Technology toward each other's potentialities, and often the lack of any attempt to reverse the situation. It is estimated that over 70 percent of the companies believe in letting both Business and Technology do their own bidding, independent of each other, unmindful of the latent *combined* potential, which would enable them to tap into the vast opportunities opened by BITA, especially in this Digital Age. What a waste!

Quite often, Technology is not even a part of the Business interactions with customers in the presales stage, even in high-tech companies. Isn't this amazing, considering that the product/technology under advisement is going to be rolled out, customized, and supported for its lifetime by the Technology teams? These companies place their trust in *hand-overs* from Business to Technology, not *alignment* between Business and Technology. It is rare to see Technology being leveraged for business, even in today's digitally dominated world where business hinges heavily on technology solutions. I would attribute this to steep functional barriers, which clog mindsets. For a business to succeed in today's digital environment, irrespective of the sector in which it operates, such barriers must be comprehensively demolished.

Example 3.1

A few years ago, a large multinational company in the high-tech software products domain—of which I was an existing client for one of their flagship products—approached me to discuss an upgrade to a more advanced system. I had been thinking of this anyway, as the existing system was already a decade old and cracking at the edges.

I arranged for them to make a presentation to our extended team, including Business folks from our company. On the appointed day, a team of presales people arrived for a two-hour presentation to us on the virtues of their new system. It was a great product pitch with some innovative slideware, designed to dazzle even the most skeptical among its audience.

Toward the end of the presentation, I asked them if they could present a slide that showed our existing system with its gaps and pain areas, and then explain how their solution helped fill these gaps? After all, that was what we were looking for as customers. It turned out that all they had was this beautiful but canned product presentation, which made no attempt to map itself to a customer's unique environment. My question was not convincingly answered, and the meeting closed with some mumblings from the account manager on the need to consult his technology team and reconvene in a few days.

This is a classic example of the Business team of a high-tech company making no attempt to engage their own support and delivery (i.e.,

---

Technology) teams in the customer presentations. Had they done so, my questions would have been quickly answered, as this company's delivery folks were working with us for years on change requests, enhancements, bug fixes, version upgrades, and so on, and knew as much about the pain points as any of my people.

Incidentally, the company above lost the deal to a competitor, which did engage its delivery team to do a short gap analysis project before making a directed pitch to us.

Two important corollaries: (1) A product, however alluring, will have an appeal for the customer only if it solves the customers' real problems, and not some imagined or case-study situations that most sellers dwell upon. (2) A cohesive front to a customer enhances your deal prospects manifold.

It is not easy to attribute business failure to the absence of BITA. When a root cause analysis is done to determine the reasons for an order loss, BITA is frequently glossed over. This happens because, in organizations still afflicted by industrial era thinking, no one *expects* BITA to work a magic in the first place, so how can *failure* be attributed to it? Deep down, this attitude has its roots in the company's siloed organization structure, preventing the pooling of ideas, skills, and knowledge. Siloes are probably the cause of more damage through missed opportunities than any single factor in the organizational framework.[3] There is a pressing need to bridge the Business and Technology functions into a connected body capable of leveraging the opportunities opened by the digital economy.

Example 3.2

For a reputed software company whose products touch millions across the globe, there was an opportunity to close a deal for a cloud-based enterprise solution. This would assure good recurring revenues for the company. The client was in touch with the company's account manager who was internally championing the deal (he narrated this incident). Before placing the order, the client wanted to understand how the technical issues around the integration of the product would be handled. The account manager told the customer that this information would need to be obtained from the technical support center and that he would follow-up with them. The process required a detailed study of the existing systems, and the client asked to get the technical folks flown down to the site for a spot assessment. The account manager had to explain that this would not be possible, since the technical support kicked in only after the deal, and not before. They would not work on, or travel for, pre-deal work. The technical support team was obviously in a silo that prevented them from looking at anything outside their cast-in-concrete charter. Approvals from upstairs might have worked the trick but would have entailed lengthy justifications. A nimbler company, with a good but lesser known product, was quick to seize the opportunity and walk away with the deal. Customers have little patience with vendors' internal bottlenecks. They have options, and your reputation can only help you thus far. If you don't get it right the first time, customers take it to mean that you never will.

BITA is a lot more than a handy tool for deal closure. The relationship with a customer starts well before the closure of a deal and goes much beyond it. BITA plays a crucial role in enhancing the *lifetime value of a customer* by fostering an increase in customer loyalty leading to upsells, repeat orders, referrals, and ultimately, business growth. But even those are mere ancillaries. A strong BITA is no longer about creating an edge in the market. It is about ensuring survival. If culture is the bedrock and strategy the blueprint, structure is the framework of BITA. A BITA-driven structure thus provides the stability needed to stay relevant and strong.

An absence of BITA often leads to (or perhaps is a result of) an atmosphere of mutual suspicion, mistrust, blame, angst, and disrespect—all of which in turn lead to the organization becoming more vulnerable to external forces, including competition. On the other hand, organizations that are built for BITA approach their common mission with a shared sense of urgency in an atmosphere of mutual trust and collaboration and can consistently deliver substantial customer (and hence shareholder) value. The question is, how does one "build for BITA"? The answer, of course, lies in *developing* exceptional talent, *organizing* it for high performance, and *aligning* it with the shared mission. We will explore these facets in some detail in this chapter.

Talent exists at the intersection of the right skills and a winning attitude (Figure 3.1). It is this *combination* of skills and attitude that enables some companies to perform unflinchingly through the storms of change, ambiguity, and complexity. As business has metamorphosed from the industrial age into the Digital Age, the contours of talent have also undergone a sea change. Someone who was a great success in an earlier era may find himself or herself quite at sea when immersed in the current digitally dominated environment (the converse is also true, but irrelevant).

As Jim Collins said in his epic book, *Good to Great*,[4] to build a successful organization, the best leaders first get the right people on the bus. That is, people with the abilities *and* temperament (in one word, *talent*) to brave the journey. They also get the wrong people *off* the bus, and quickly. Finally, they assign the right seats on the bus to the right people.

Let us begin with the new-age *attitudes* necessary for BITA. Attitudes, unlike skills, are not shaped by functions and roles and are regarded as inherent. A given set of attitudes pervades the organization as its *culture*. Today, what you can do is a lot more important than who you are. Your ability and drive to deliver results matter far more than your function, role, or level. Organizations must, therefore, strive to ingrain the right set of *attitudes* that characterize Digital Age professionalism for driving business value.

The question is, what is this right set of attitudes? Contrary to popular belief, attitudes are not inborn and *can* be acquired. True, we are born with specific characteristics in our DNA, while others are deeply etched through our upbringing, and so on. But it is possible to *build* certain attitudes, given the right climate. The rub-off effect works well in transmitting

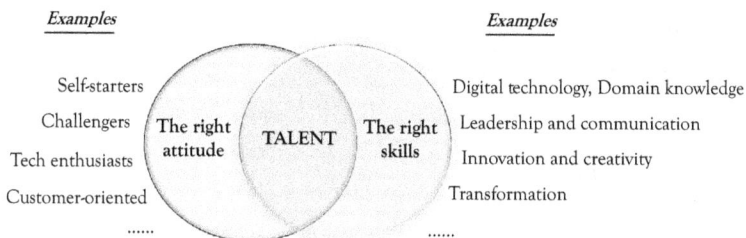

Figure 3.1 Talent

or uncovering attitudinal traits. If we are in a high-energy zone where everyone is passionate about results, we tend to acquire a sense of urgency, which may not have surfaced in a different, less demanding setting.

Fostering the right attitudes for success in the Digital Age, through edification or onboarding, is of far-reaching consequence and cannot be compromised. If you must, compromise with skills, they can be acquired. Attitudes are much harder to develop. There is no universal set of attitudes that one must look to maximize, but certain traits do play an important role for a healthy BITA, as we shall see.

Example 3.3

Sometimes, a positive attitude compensates more than adequately for even the biggest blunders. I was on a two-day business trip to Chennai and was staying at a hotel where most folks traveling from my company routinely did, though it was a first for me. I had had a particularly hard and long day at the office, and I was quite tired and beat when I hit the bed that night, hoping to catch a restful and undisturbed sleep. It was not to be. Promptly at 4.00 a.m., there was the sound of the doorbell, accompanied by knocks on the door, which woke me up. It took me a while to get my bearings and walk unsteadily to the door. On opening it, I found a smartly dressed waiter, somehow looking fresh and crisp even at that unearthly hour, smiling ear-to-ear, deftly holding a tea-tray laden with a kettle, cup and a rose. In a sing-song voice, he cheerily wished me a good morning. "This is your wake-up call, sir. I hope you have a pleasant flight back and a great day ahead," he announced, smiling broadly throughout the exchange. Now, I had given no wake-up call, nor had any flights to catch until evening that day. But his whole demeanor was such that even after the obvious discomfort of having my sleep interrupted, I didn't have the heart to chastise him or disappoint him by refusing the tea. I took it from him, thanked him sleepily, and went back to sleep. Had it been a less positive attitude, it would not have drowned my irritability. I would have undoubtedly raised the matter in a firm voice with him, and even more firmly with his management, and generally, the day would not have gone well for him. But his attitude changed mine. I let it go.

> *It was only on waking up at about 8.00 a.m. that I realized that the price of this early and sweet exchange was probably paid by an unfortunate soul somewhere in the hotel who missed his flight that morning! It was too late to do anything about it, and I just let it pass, but with a little twinge of guilt ...*

On the other hand, people tend to take a less charitable view of those who possess sharp skills but do not have an attitude to match. Again, best explained with an example.

Example 3.4

A telecom company had commissioned a Wi-Fi network at a busy airport. The system was designed to offer Wi-Fi to thousands of passengers during wait periods, and in the process, improve the airport's service quality index (SQI). The Wi-Fi service became very popular, and data traffic soon peaked to full capacity. But at these high-traffic loads, the system performance became somewhat erratic, and many user complaints started coming in relating to poor experiences. Wi-Fi became one of the root causes of plummeting SQI. When news of this reached the airport CEO, he summoned the company for a discussion on the subject. A team consisting of their business unit head, the account manager, and a technical expert walked into the CEO's office where he and a few of his operations folks were waiting for them. When the CEO started relating the problem, the technical expert suddenly became vocal and launched off into an intricate sermon, which consisted of terms and concepts that no one could grasp. He was clearly of the view that by flaunting expert knowledge, he was creating a positive impression and earning some respect. After a few minutes, the CEO stopped him and plainly said that he didn't quite understand the technical jargon. To which this guy smugly replied that people who deploy technology must first make an attempt to understand it!

To make matters worse, the "expert" then suggested a series of causes that pointed the blame to the customer. He thought it was his duty to deflect the blame from his company! Protestations from the airport operations guys present in the meeting only amplified the charges. A point was reached when the CEO could take it no longer. He called an end to the meeting and asked the company folks to leave, while also instructing his team members present to find an alternative quickly. The business head somehow reasoned with the CEO to allow them to stay and find a solution together. The CEO relented but insisted on this expert being shown out of the room, which he was. Luckily for the company, they could arrive at a course of action, which resulted in the current problems being satisfactorily addressed and their staying in the reckoning for the nationwide expansion project that was in the offing here.

This expert was a master of his game. Highly skilled, he had technology at his fingertips. But this gave him a supercilious attitude, leading him to believe that his conduct in that meeting was "professional."

While technical skills are indeed valuable, their manifestation in the above manner is the reason many companies score low on BITA. For professionals in the Digital Age, great skills without the right attitude are like yin without yang—incomplete.

Attitude is tough to generalize, and we all have our own brand of it that we share with no one. Still, BITA calls for some very characteristic traits that were quite alien to, say, the industrial age. Of course, there is a *foundational* base of primeval traits that the new-age work attitudes are built upon, like uncompromising work ethic, excellence orientation, customer centricity, and so on. But these must be *supplemented* by an entirely new set of attitudes unique to the digital enterprise. The talent pool that is going to steer you to success in the new economy will be defined by all the following attitudes, however uncharacteristic it may seem from your current standpoint.

- Youthful (in spirit if not in age)
- Insanely energetic
- Value creativity
- Take risks (dare-to-try)
- Positive spirited. Take failure in their stride
- Go-getters. Stretch themselves for accomplishing their mission
- Love new technologies

- Believe in direct and unambiguous communication (both ways)
- Openly ambitious
- Get bored in a static setting
- Self-starters. Do not like to be supervised
- Always on the lookout for new challenges (May quit their jobs sooner)
- Agile and unbounded. Not restrained by functional boundaries and office decorum

For the striving digital enterprise, this is clearly the stuff of Spartan warriors (Chapter 2). Does this define you?

Let's turn to the other ingredient of the talent pie—the skills. These are somewhat easier to mold and cultivate than attitudes but are no less important. There are two important differences: One, most skills are realm or function-dependent, and two, skills are layered, built progressively

At the bottom layer of the skills stack are the unique *occupational* skills like programming skills for software developers, PMP certification for project managers, accountancy for banking professionals, trading acumen for investment advisors, network planning for telecom engineers, and so on. There is nothing transformative about occupational skills. From the ancient ages to the present, they have been central to the vocational agenda. Apparently, while these may be necessary, they are not *enough* for distinction in the new age.

Skills must be progressive. No doubt demand continues to be vibrant for MBAs who can crunch numbers, lawyers who can craft contracts, and programmers who can crank code. But if this is all that defines you as a professional, your career ladder could be a rather short one. As you progress, the needle must move from skills that emphasize repetitive tasks (like coding and testing) to skills that emphasize higher order abilities (like creativity and analysis). At the very top, the emphasis is on *human ability* that is *beyond the power of computerization or automation to replicate.* Therefore, skills like creativity, pattern recognition, trend spotting, storytelling and synopsizing, empathy, and discernment (*meaning* making) are among the real *differentiators* that must be fostered in the digital era. These and other *human* skills will acquire much greater significance as information and intelligence will increasingly become the domain of *computers.*

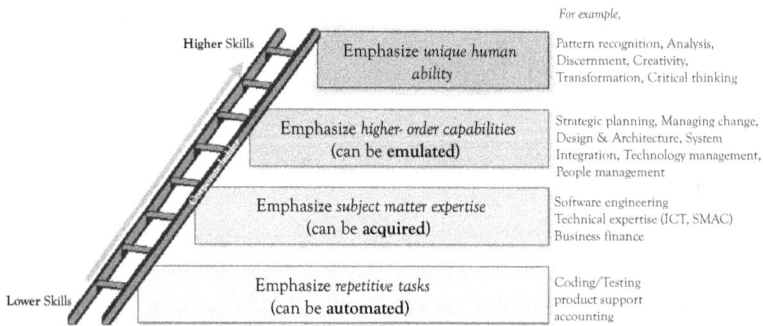

Figure 3.2 Skills progression

> **Exercise:** *Specific to your industry, identify the most desirable skills in each of the four boxes shown against the corporate ladder (Figure 3.2), from the lowermost skills to the highest skills. Where do you see yourself today on this ladder? In five years?*

The main propulsion for BITA comes from its people, who are defined by the skills and attitudes that they bring to work. Therefore, compromising on these while focusing on the other dimensions would be like attempting to run a swanky car on an empty fuel tank.

In my experience, I have had the opportunity to be part of the hiring process for professionals at every level. The right focus during the hiring process obviously has a lot to do with building exceptional teams. However, it is not always easy to pick the best based on job interviews, and mistakes happen. Some can be addressed through counseling, training, rotation, and so on, while others have less agreeable remedies. It is possible to minimize the possibility of hiring error if your focus is on multiple dimensions, resulting in a more comprehensive assessment. Most mistakes occur because we hire based on technical (or subject) knowledge alone, perhaps giving some fleeting importance to visible traits like demeanor and deportment. Your assessment must cover *all* the following attributes, especially for full-time hires who will be looking for opportunities to grow in due course.

- Domain competence
- Strategic thinking

- Execution excellence
- Business/customer orientation
- Technology orientation
- Interpersonal effectiveness
- Learning orientation
- Teamwork and alignment
- Lateral thinking (innovation)

As one moves up the ladder, the *nondomain* attributes assume progressively higher significance, though the importance of domain competence is not entirely diminished. In general, skills at the lower rungs are more amenable to automation. There is also greater scope here for outsourcing to like-minded third parties. Enterprises must invest in creating a structure which takes these factors into account while building organizational stability. From the standpoint of the Technology team, sizing up the *Business* architecture (structure, functions, information needs), creating a business-aligned *Technology* structure, and developing detailed job description sheets stating the business purpose and requirement for each position, must precede the actual hiring process.

The Functions of Technology (IT)

The mission of Technology is to enable business success. Accordingly, Technology must assure that the organization can *run* business operations [R], and *change*, develop, or transform business systems [C] to *achieve the business mission*. Following are some of the typical functions of Technology:

- Design and deploy a scalable IT architecture and IT systems to support current and future business requirements [R]
- Manage internal and external operational support systems including hardware, software, network, and information security with a high degree of availability and recovery [R]
- Manage the company's data and information as an enterprise asset [R]

- Enable uninterrupted access to ICT applications, information, and tools including CRM, ERP, and enterprise applications [R]
- Design, development, implementation, and support of software applications and enhancements [C]
- Optimizing processes by collaborating with Business to define Business Process Reengineering (BPR) strategy to achieve efficiencies [C]
- Planning, execution, and delivery of customer projects [C]
- Technical solution consulting—internal (e.g., presales) and external [C]
- Thought leadership to the Business on technology direction and potential, as a strategic advisor [C]

Exercise: Can you list all the functions of Technology in your organization and categorize them as [R] or [C]? Is your Technology function more run-dominated, or change-dominated?

When we refer to the alignment of Technology with Business, we imply that all Technology functions, including the above, are operating in synchronization and harmony with Business.

Business Structure

Here is a very quick dip-stick check to test the alignment between Business and Technology in your organization. Ask a few of your Technology team members to explain the broad structure of the Business organization in your company. Likely, you will find that most people will be unable to give a satisfactory answer to this seemingly simple question. You will probably get similarly vague answers if you ask the Business team members about the Technology organization. Even though it is true in most organizations, this is rather disturbing from a BITA perspective. How on earth can two organizations that do not even recognize each other's form and function ever hope to align?

An understanding of the Business structure is not a matter of choice for the Technology team. The Business structure, in fact, is the very basis of the Technology structure. An organization that builds a Technology structure disconnected from the Business will find the going quite rough on its digital journey, and at some point will go down the ravine.

Unfortunately, there is no standard Business organization and hence no fixed Business structure. Depending on whether you *produce, provide, deliver,* or—as is becoming common in the Digital Age—*aggregate* goods and services, you may have Business structures that are widely different. Similarly, your structure would vary to reflect whether you are a local, regional, or global enterprise, serving consumers or enterprises.

The essential point is that for BITA to exist, the Technology organization must invest in understanding the organization's Business structure, including key *strategic focus areas* like business lines, major functions, geographies, and channels, as shown in Figure 3.3a. The understanding must include knowledge of the key people, processes, and priorities. While the greater the depth of understanding the better, it may not always be possible for the Technology organization to master all nuances that make up the Business organization. This is fine. A general view pervading the Technology organization works for BITA.

Figure 3.3a is a rather simplistic and high-level picture of a Business organization. In one of its possible enactments [3-3(b)], the business regions may be organized as *verticals* and other blocks as *horizontals* supporting some or all the verticals. The endeavor of the Technology organization must be to have clarity on *at least the relevant Independent Business Units (IBUs)* in Figure 3.3 to be able to engage more closely and drive alignment. For example, who are the key people associated with the function of Business Intelligence (BI) and what are their immediate and longer-term priorities? Good Technology (IT) organizations have *business analysts* for going *deeper* into the Business organization to drive the integration between Business and Technology.

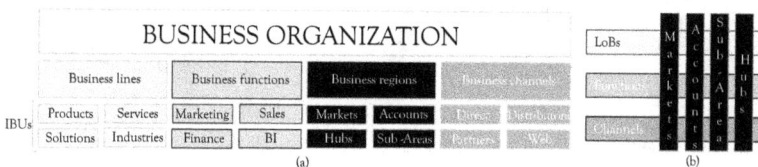

Figure 3.3 Schematic of business organization

Technology Structure

Technology (IT) too does not have a standard mold in which all structures fit. A Technology organization that aims to align with Business, however, starts with certain distinct characteristics that it does not relinquish through its journey, in smooth times or tumultuous.

A Business-aligned Technology structure is based on the premise that for achieving success together, Business and Technology must *think*, *build*, and *operate* as one. This must manifest in the structure and not just be confined to spirit. For most of its history, Technology has been a tool for achieving office productivity gains and automation of linear processes. Its role as a *Business enabler* is only now evolving; hence, most enterprises must make a concerted effort to reflect this in the structure.

IT started as a shared service (stage 1 in Figure 3.4) for providing and supporting common infrastructure like LAN and PCs to create a more efficient work environment. It had no direct role in the growth of the business. In stage 2, IT became an agency for *automating* specific business processes, where it developed (or *Built*) software programs for Business, though still a lot of area is uncovered in terms of *optimizing* processes because Business and IT were still not *thinking* together. Nor were they *operating* in concert, save for some IT operational support to Business by way of maintenance.

Next, in stage 3, IT evolves to become a productivity enhancer for the Business. IT is no longer responsible for merely automating existing processes, but also for *tuning* those processes to achieve greater efficiencies. IT also shares more space with Business in the operations sphere by

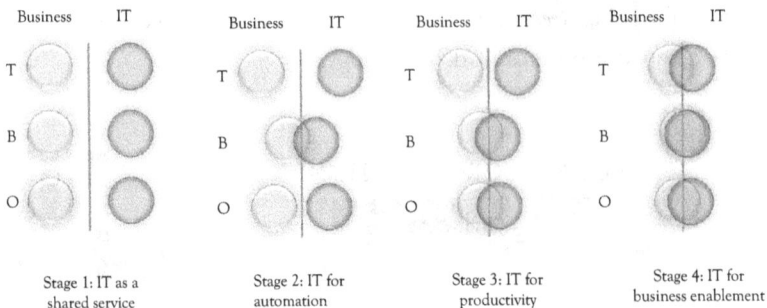

| Stage 1: IT as a shared service | Stage 2: IT for automation | Stage 3: IT for productivity | Stage 4: IT for business enablement |

Figure 3.4 Evolving role of IT in the enterprise

enabling a secure and productive environment for Business, helping it to launch better and faster solutions to surpass time-to-market requirements, and extending services toward improving customer experience.

In stage 4, Business and IT cross over the boundary into each other's territory to think, build, and operate together. It is here that BITA happens. Business and IT are now equal stakeholders in the creation of business value. In this stage, IT as a thought leader does not just implement Business-defined solutions but is one with Business in imagining and creating solutions that would help the Business *and its customers* stay ahead—now and in the future. Business has visibility and influence over the IT architecture, while IT is tuned into the competitive landscape to derive its priorities from it. Business and IT have equal participation in the development of solutions, having a common view of the time, cost, and quality of builds. IT understands the business processes, and is an advisor to the Business on their optimization and enhancement to outdo industry best practices. A *complete* overlap—like a total eclipse—would overshadow either Business or IT and severely restrict individuality. Therefore, for alignment, a *reasonable* overlap is sought, leaving room for independence of thought and action.

The elements that constitute Business and IT thinking, building, and operating together are reproduced in Table 3.1 for ready reference. For example, an overlap in the *Plan* attribute would mean that Business and Technology have an unwavering practice of *jointly* deciding and delivering on the *strategy* and *roadmap* and are aligned on the responsibilities and implications that it entails. And so on.

Table 3.1 TBO attributes

Aspect	Associated attributes
Think	**Plan**—Strategy, Roadmap I **Design**—Innovation, Improvement I **Share**—Knowledge, Ideas, Culture I **Measure**—Trends, Analysis
Build	**Collaborate**—Governance, Teamwork, Partnerships I **Construct**—Process, Organization I **Deliver**—Projects, Solutions I **Deploy**—Technology, Best practices I **Optimize**—Time, Cost, Quality
Operate	**Execute**—Sell, Service, Install I **Monitor**—Performance, Cost, Process I **Control**—Assets, Policies I **Support**—Customer experience, enterprise productivity, data privacy, and security

Our next task is to assure that the Technology *organization structure* is right for BITA. As there could be several manifestations of Technology, each with its own variables, there cannot be a single, universally applicable organogram. The unifying factor is the underlying intention to think, build, and operate as one with the Business.

The terms think, build, and operate are not units or functions in themselves, nor do they ascribe specific behaviors to individuals. Thus, it is not that only people assigned to the Think band do the thinking, and others don't! The roles and functions ascribed to the Think band are chosen for their aptitude to interwork with the Business to *conceptualize* what it takes to achieve success together. The roles and functions of the Build band are chosen to *develop* together per this blueprint, while the roles and functions in the Operate band are chosen to *sustain* the alignment for long-term success.

Figure 3.5 is a depiction of one possible *Business-aligned IT organization structure*. The essence of this structure is that it enables the different independent business units (IBUs) to leverage all the functions of IT through a dedicated IT interface, which is the business analyst. It splits the IT functions and roles into bands to enable Business and IT to think, build, and operate with a common mission while upholding the modularity of the structure. You can, for example, replace specific roles in this structure without disturbing the other functions or the overall alignment with Business. Similarly, if the business expands to include more IBUs, it does not require a material change in the supporting IT structure.

In a more general sense, an IBU refers to a sub-function within business, as in Figure 3.3. For example, in the case of banking business, an

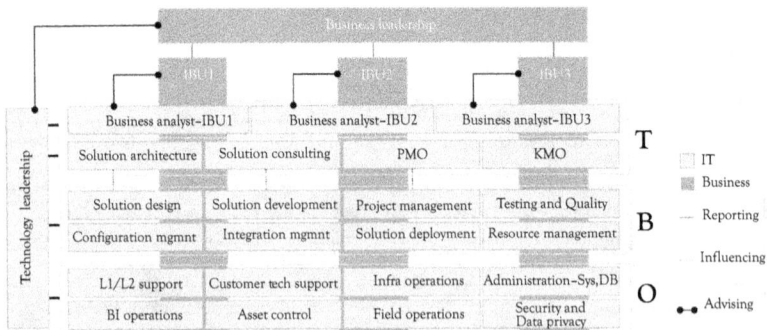

Figure 3.5 Example of IT organization structure

IBU could be the merchant banking unit or the retail (personal) banking unit. In the case of a software development company, the various IBUs could be designated by the different industry verticals such as banking, financial services, and insurance (BFSI), and telecom. In some environments, an IBU represents a large customer account—as in the case of telecom equipment vendors, or consulting firms. To sum up, an IBU is a distinct but synergistic unit of business within a business, having its own strategic focus. As a first step, *the Technology organization needs to identify and understand the IBUs* in operation within the company.

Let us walk through the various TBO functions to comprehend their role in developing a Business-aligned IT structure.

THINK

The Think band is primarily concerned with envisioning the outcomes that would increase the value created by the enterprise. The Think band sets the stage for developing alignment between Business and IT to drive innovation, sharing of knowledge, and design of solutions, methods, and measurement systems for enterprise transformation. Key roles here are Business Analyst, Solution Consultant, Solution Architect, Program Management Office (PMO), and Knowledge Management Office (KMO). A business analyst (BA) is typically assigned to *each* IBU in a *dedicated* way as an ambassador of Technology while being a champion of his IBU within Technology. That is, the BA is the single point of contact for the Business, who pools the combined strength of the entire Technology organization in support of his IBU. This effectively addresses the prime business concern of *whom to contact* for an IT matter. [The term BA is not universal; this role can have other titles like Business Information Officer, Business Consultant, or IT Account manager.]

BUILD

The Build band represents the region where ideas get materialized into products and solutions that are of value to the enterprise and its customers. The Build band includes roles related to the development, testing, integration, and deployment of products, services, and solutions. It also includes creation of a framework for managing and governing projects, processes, and structure of IT. It, therefore, has a vital role in digital transformation of the enterprise. The new-age digital environment is a dynamic one, characterized by changing customer aspirations and technological evolution, necessitating a tuning of the organization framework (processes, capabilities, structure). Further, it is not an environment where one size fits all and requires several parallel, personalized versions of a solution to be developed. These are the primary reasons for new-age digital enterprises adopting the *iterative* or *agile* model of development, in which Business and Technology are *required* to be always and fully intertwined. Projects get into trouble when, after the initial estimation, everyone except the project delivery team is hands-off. In some businesses, like a software development company, the Build overlap extends beyond the company's business group to its customers.

OPERATE

The Digital Age has brought some de-facto alignment between Business and Technology at the Think and Build levels, but it is still quite rare to see this extend to the Operate level. Considering that the Operate level functions mainly in the customers' line of sight, this is indeed awkward. Organizations that demonstrate alignment at the Operate level, however, score better on customer experience parameters. Critical functions in the Operate band include rendering an enriched experience throughout the customer lifecycle, managing essential infrastructure and optimizing its cost and performance to meet business plans, and very importantly, assuring confidentiality, integrity, and availability of business information by building a secure IT environment. All these functions have an impact on business sustainability and customer loyalty. In other words, a structure that underplays the importance of alignment at the Operate level is often responsible for business erosion and customer churn.

Job Specifications Sheet

A job specifications sheet is generally used as a template for hiring new employees. It is also a handy reference sheet for understanding the role of peer employees in other functions, thus improving the chances of alignment. Instead of being cloaked in confidentiality, a job specifications sheet must, therefore, be published on the company intranet for maximum visibility. While it is not pertinent for everyone to understand each nuance of every role, it does help to gain an insight into the purpose, charter, and interfaces of the roles that you are expected to align with. For example, it would be meaningful for a presales executive from Business to understand the role of a solution consultant in IT, and vice-versa.

A job sheet assures objectivity, uniformity, and transparency in the hiring process, making it less susceptible to individual notions. Further, it is essential to review and reassess the job specifications with changes in the business environment.

One possible format of a job specification sheet for any given role, like an IT Business Analyst, is shown in Figure 3.6.

A well-prepared job specification sheet gives a reasonably clear view of what can be expected from a given role. It would, however, be reckless to close the section on job specification sheets without emphasizing that a job specification is only a *guideline*, and when the need of the hour is to step out for a larger goal, the incumbent is willing and ready to do it. Roles are not rigid, and unlike rules, may be bent.

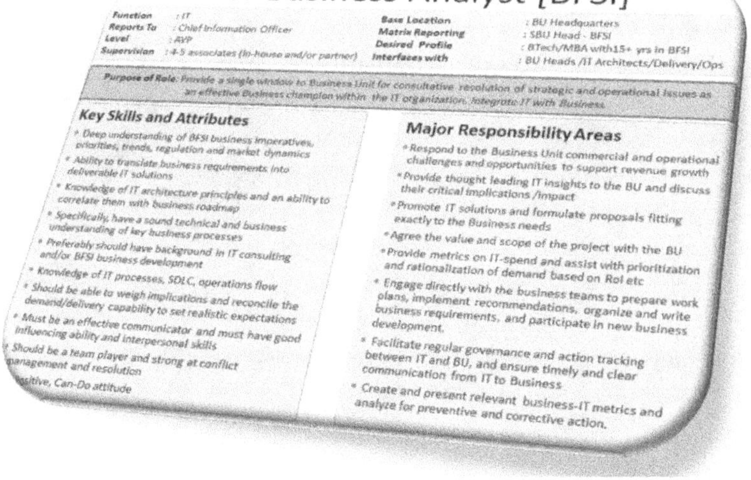

Figure 3.6 Job description sheet

Job-Skills Assessment

BITA is not a spark that is required to ignite the enterprise into traction, but rather the combustion that keeps the organization in continual motion over smooth as well as rough terrain. Accordingly, certain methodologies have evolved to assess the individual's developmental needs periodically to reaffirm conformance to BITA requirements and institute developmental actions to ensure that BITA is sustained in the enterprise.

This process must not be confused with the performance management system. It is *not* required to follow a bell curve or a ranking system, and its purpose is to *develop*, not appraise.

Well-defined job descriptions, business plans, and KRAs are of little use if they fail to set the rhythm for the people in the organization to advance toward their mission. Sustained Business–Technology alignment

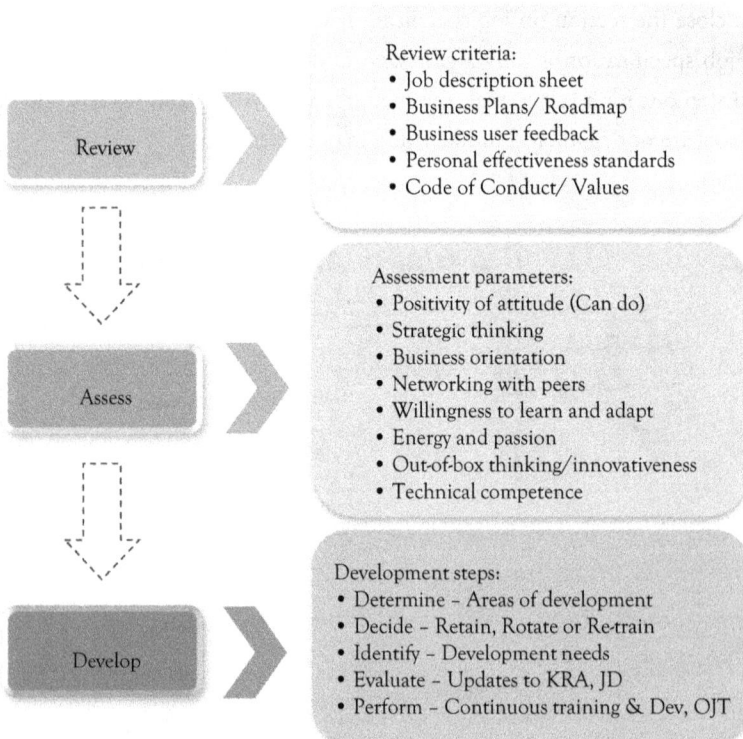

Review

Review criteria:
- Job description sheet
- Business Plans/ Roadmap
- Business user feedback
- Personal effectiveness standards
- Code of Conduct/ Values

Assess

Assessment parameters:
- Positivity of attitude (Can do)
- Strategic thinking
- Business orientation
- Networking with peers
- Willingness to learn and adapt
- Energy and passion
- Out-of-box thinking/innovativeness
- Technical competence

Develop

Development steps:
- Determine – Areas of development
- Decide – Retain, Rotate or Re-train
- Identify – Development needs
- Evaluate – Updates to KRA, JD
- Perform – Continuous training & Dev, OJT

Figure 3.7 Job-skills assessment

requires that clear assessment parameters are defined for each role, against which developmental needs are continually assessed. In Figure 3.7, some *generic* assessment parameters (AP) that are important from a BITA perspective are presented. Companies may evolve their own systems for this assessment. In general, it is preferred to assess individuals on a 1–5 scale on each AP, based on a composite of informal interviews by a neutral agency, track-record as briefed by the supervisor, and feedback from peers and stakeholders through informal chats (templated feedback forms are not a good idea here as most people are very reserved in giving inputs that could become a matter of record, especially about their colleagues and peers). In most situations, engaging an external consultant works best.

Finally, one may create a simple radar graph as shown in Figure 3.8, which displays the individual's average assessment scores against the target fixed for each position/ experience level. Here, we have plotted the chart for John Doe, Solution Consultant. The assessment parameters and targets may also be made specific to roles, drawn directly from the job description.

This display makes it easy to identify the strengths (which is Technical Competence for John Doe) and development needs (like Willingness to Learn). Such graphs may be created yearly to assess the individual's progress against defined APs.

Having determined the developmental needs, you may ascertain the best course of action, including learning programs, on-the-job training, mentoring, or refitment of the individual in another role.

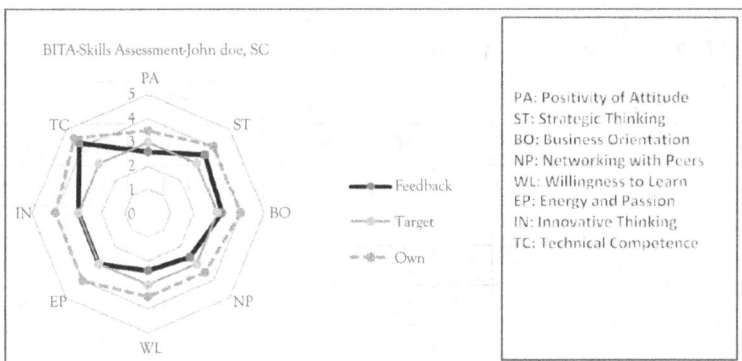

Figure 3.8 Individual skills assessment scorecard

Example 3.5

Several years ago, I was a general manager at the R&D center in India of a reputable global organization in the telecommunications space. My team consisted of very talented people taken from top institutes and the best peer companies. The nature of the work put a very heavy emphasis not just on picking the right skills but continually upgrading them to keep up with the complex dynamics and rigors of global R&D. The process of competency review, assessment, and development was, therefore, well-institutionalized in the organization as a best practice.

In time, the parent company in the United States divested chunks of its portfolio to other companies. My unit was acquired by a large multinational technology company, which saw a great opportunity in this acquisition. The competency levels of our people who had joined their ranks stood out as a clear strategic differentiator, which would be of great value in their mission of achieving global leadership.

The management of the new company saw significant value in the competency assessment system at work in the acquired unit, finding it neutral, transparent, and repeatable. This was institutionalized in the new environment to quickly match the attributes of an individual with the requirements of roles and programs, and to create synergy and balance between the acquiring company's existing workforce and the new joiners from the acquired unit. An updated Competency Assessment Card (as shown in Table 3.2) was maintained for every individual, which was used to build aligned project teams.

Table 3.2 **Competency Assessment Card**

JANE SMITH	SC			65-362				
(Photo)	PA	ST	BO	NP	WL	EP	IN	TC
External Interviewer	3.0	2.5	2.5	4.0	3.5	3.5	2.5	3.0
Manager	3.0	3.0	3.5	3.5	4.0	3.0	3.0	3.0
Peer-1	3.5	2.5	2.5	3.5	3.5	2.6	2.5	2.5
Peer-2	3.5	2.5	3.0	4.5	4.0	4.0	3.5	3.5
Self	4.0	3.5	3.5	4.0	4.0	4.0	4.0	4.0
Overall Score	3.4	2.8	3.0	3.9	3.8	3.4	3.1	3.2

> *The Business teams were the first to reap the benefits as faster time-to-market, better quality, and more innovation in customer-solution showed up in the results. The company has since "digitized" the process. Inputs are fed directly by each reviewer, which the system collates to match job skills to relevant project requirements.*

Structure as a Driver of Personal and Organizational Growth

A sound structure reinforces the organization by providing direction and scope for personal growth to the people of the organization. There are five significant advantages that a good structure offers to every individual who is a part of it, as in Table 3.3.

Table 3.3 Structure advantages

Commitment	Passion and enthusiasm to deliver on assigned responsibilities
Development	Opportunities to learn and grow
Alignment	Oneness with the larger organization
Empowerment	Freedom to think and act
Achievement	Motivation to excel

If you are unable to realize the apparent gains in spite of overall job-skills assessment being positive, it is probable that some *archaic practices are inhibiting the people from delivering to their full potential.*

Organizations that overlooked these inhibitors have witnessed their structures implode upon themselves, despite a solid foundation.

Inhibitors, as depicted in Figure 3.9, are one of the major blocking factors of personal and organizational growth. To identify these, invite feedback from folks, either in team meetings or through online polling, at least once in a year, on unpopular practices in your organization. You may get some mischievous responses that need to be filtered out, but you will also get some relevant inputs worth acting upon. The overarching goal of this exercise is to provide a productive and conducive environment for people to exploit their full potential, *without compromising on the organizational code of conduct.* Here are a few general pointers on restrictive practices, but I would urge you to create a list that is specific to your

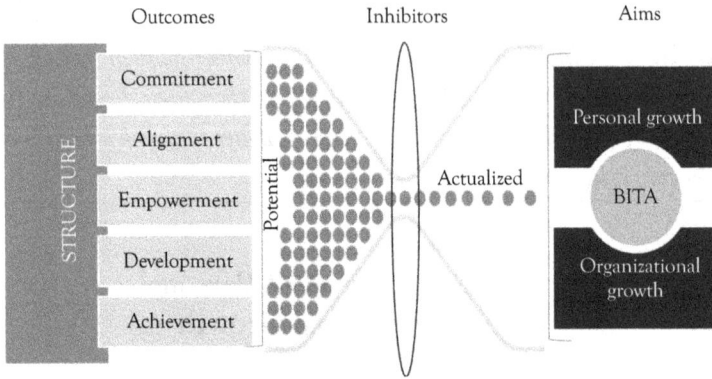

Figure 3.9 Inhibitors to personal and organizational growth

environment before deciding on the practices to be modified or phased out.

1. Keeping people chained to a role because the policy requires a minimum term (say one year) to be completed before a job rotation can be considered. This serves no purpose if the person is better suited to the other position *and* is motivated to move there.
2. Fitting people into a forced bell curve. Companies that force people into a statistical distribution invoke insecurities even in the best people.
3. Restricting the use of the Internet in the office. How can blocking information in the information age be productive? A workforce that has the *freedom* to stay connected is a much happier and more motivated workforce than a restricted one.
4. A governance system built on command, control, and acquiescence. This could range from strict policies enforcing style and format of communication, requiring approvals for almost everything, and even curbing the freedom to keep personal memorabilia like photos on office desk (because it *distracts*). One of the reasons why companies like Google and Apple are rated as top places to work is that they have not embraced such systems.
5. Inflexibility regarding timings, hours, and workplace. This is an industrial age hangover when card punching machines were installed

at factory gates, with wages linked to work hours. Today, what you achieve is a lot more important than how many hours you worked, or from where you worked (home or office).

6. An undue emphasis on a formal decorum. In this age where a large part of the workforce is in their 20s, organizations that lay too much emphasis on old-school decorum—like following strict protocol in approaching senior leadership, respecting closed doors, and so on—are only distancing themselves from their workforce. Ideas flow best when people are in their comfort zones.

These are only a few out of dozens of value-subtracting practices. You may like to prepare a fuller list of the practices in your own company that cause frustration and demotivation while achieving nothing of value. Many of these retrograde rituals are not only injurious to the morale of the people but are also a millstone around BITA. How can alignment happen when people are neither inspired nor free to express themselves?

A digital enterprise is nothing but the *collective* capacity of its people to create value. As we saw in this chapter, close alignment between Business and Technology is critical to building this capacity for sustained competitive advantage.

CHAPTER 4

The Process Paradigm

"There are two ways to do something—the right way, and again."

Example 4.1

A few years ago, I was in Malaysia for discussing a large customer relationship management (CRM) transformation deal with a big corporation, along with members of our consortium. It was an intense week of research and customer meetings during the days, followed by preparations, discussions, and synchronization among consortium members late into the nights.

On the final day, there was a dinner event with all the consortium members and the customer's senior team. During this event, the customer's CIO addressed us to express thanks on behalf of her organization to all the people who had traveled from India, Sri Lanka, and Australia and spent the week working with her teams on scoping out the new project, identifying gaps, and presenting solutions. She went on to say that she and her team had learned a great deal from us on the value of Business and Technology teams working together and delivering so much more than they could have done individually. The other senior executives present reiterated these sentiments, expressing that our aligned approach was like a breath of fresh air, which they hoped to see in future too. We won the deal!

Clearly, the most critical factor for the customer was the show of alignment across the constituents, and this gave us that crucial edge over some of our larger competitors who boasted of greater technological depth and price flexibility. In short, BITA at work became the key differentiator for us.

The above is a feel-good example that probably resonates with some of your own winning experiences. But what does it have to do with *process*, you may well ask? Process, as we have come to understand, is a set of conventions that *prescribe* the way a program must be implemented. Usually, this is a well-documented workflow with associated policies, forms, and templates. But there is no prescription evident in the example. So how is process alignment evidenced here? Let's explore this.

The purpose of a process is to achieve *consistency* and *efficiency* in the way *inputs* (aspirations) are converted into defined *outputs* (value). Enterprise processes may be grouped into *clusters,* as depicted in Figure 4.1.

The first process cluster is the *functional* processes. These are processes that are *internal* to a function, that is, serve the requirements of that function alone. For example, the finance function may have a process for reconciliation of vendor invoices against budget provisions, or the Technology function may have a process for periodic data center equipment maintenance. These processes, while important, operate *within* a function to improve internal efficiency, productivity, or conformity.

PROCESS ALIGNMENT

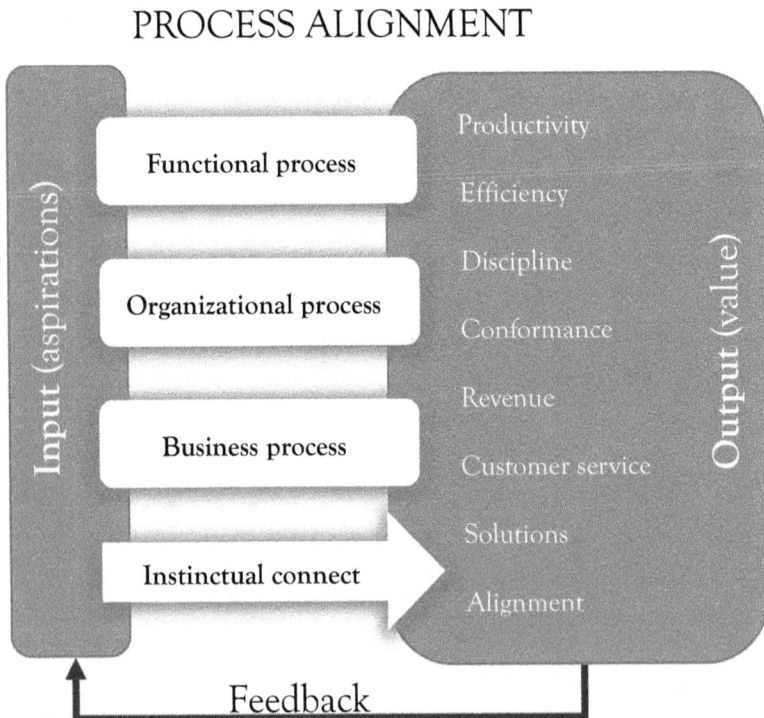

Figure 4.1 Process clusters

The next process cluster is *organizational* processes. These are processes that cut across functional boundaries to accomplish organizational aims. Examples of these are the performance management process, procurement process, software license usage and compliance process.

And finally, there are the *Business* processes–like the Billing, Customer Experience Management (CEM), Supplier Relationship Management (SRM), web/mobile based client applications, like e-commerce or self-service portal—which directly influence customer (or external stakeholder) experience and hence the *business outcome*. Business processes are usually invoked through rule-based automated workflows, which, however elegant, may be replicated by others, and this may blunt their competitive edge. Therefore, their constant sharpening is essential to stay ahead.

There is also a fourth and less acknowledged level, or perhaps a *connection*, which is *intuitive*, not rule-based. We will call this the *instinctual connect*. This also has the same goal as a process. It occurs when Business and Technology are *instinctively* aligned in such a way that each can relate to and complement the actions of the other in providing imaginative solutions in a complex environment. Creative solutions are a consequence of the *instinctual connection*, which, while respecting the defined and documented processes, leverages the *human* instincts of anticipation, pragmatism, and prudence. The example at the beginning of this chapter is an illustration of the *instinctual connection*.

The instinctual connection—unlike the functional, organizational, and business processes—is not a formal and documented system. It has no associated templates or workflows. Think of it this way: You and your friend are on a survival mission, wandering through rocky wilderness, risking wild animals, steep precipices, and falling boulders. Supplies are dwindling fast, and the safety of the base camp is still days away. In this situation, what do you rely on? You do, of course, depend on certain laid-down methods for preserving rations and keeping your gear in readiness. But most of all, you rely on each other. In short, the instinctual connect. Without a rulebook in hand, the instinctual connect allows you "to do what is right" and have each other's back. At such a time, all the written down guidelines and operating procedures have at best a marginal value in your life.

The above is an allegory for a typical business setting in the intensely competitive Digital Age. Brutal competition, unpredictability, regulatory headwinds, and resource limitations are only some of the challenges that continually test your endurance. To survive in this hostile climate, like in your rough adventure in the mountains, you must rely on something more than a set of documented processes.

Documented and prescribed procedures certainly do have a role to play in steering the enterprise. However, instinctual connect is the *lubrication* required to run the process machinery. Whether on a survival mission in the wilds or the whirlwind world of business, you need it to beat the odds. In the tumultuous world of digital business, *BITA* is your instinctual connect.

Functional Processes

Though functional processes are internal to a function, their impact may be felt beyond the function if they flop. An inconsistent sales reporting process, for example, may delay interventions, and a flawed data management process may lead to irreconciled enterprise information, both with catastrophic results for the enterprise. Functional processes, therefore, *do* have an impact on the business outcome.

In digital enterprises, business functional processes rely on Technology for their development, and hence, BITA is a substantial factor in their operation. The sales-reporting process, for example, requires Technology to understand the sales cycle to create systems for capturing, processing, and presenting relevant information, and migrating these systems to the cloud for access by a mobile sales force.

Similarly, Technology functional processes in digital enterprises rely on Business. The Technology project management process using agile software development, for example, relies on continuous inputs from Business. In a shift of stance ushered by the digital era, Business and Technology must not only understand each other's functional processes but play a crucial part in their enablement. A strong BITA is, therefore, key to getting the best out of your functional processes in the Digital Age.

Organizational Processes

Organization processes exist for institutionalizing internal procedures that impact the entire organization. Their primary focus is on bringing uniformity in the way organizational outcomes are achieved, while also guarding the enterprise against internal waywardness. Do's and don'ts in matters of recruitment, performance management, compliance to usage and licensing terms, decorum and security, and so on, are all guided by organizational processes.

Instances of some organizational processes being viewed as counterintuitive are not uncommon, particularly in the Digital Age.

Example 4.2

An IT company (no less!) had a policy that employees up to a particular salary grade must log in to their computers on reaching office, and the time of log-in would be recorded as their in-time by the Leave and Attendance Process that lapped up this information. This application was linked to the salary system, with some back-end algorithm to mark x number of accumulated late hours as full-day leave from work. If you were a sales guy who wanted to make an early morning visit to his customer before coming to the office, you would be marked late, and only after explanations and approvals from your seniors, could you regularize the entry. Employees often argued that they frequently worked much after office hours, but the system gave no credit for that, while it immediately penalized them for late coming, even for very valid reasons. The counterargument was that reversal of this process could lead to indiscipline and discrimination! The company was also worried about precedence, and this drove it to enforce this seemingly flawed process, disregarding its impact on morale. The process defied all logic, yet its proponents could keep it alive for years.

The important point here is that organizational processes are susceptible to the inertia of tradition and hence, need to be reviewed and tested for relevance periodically. Many of these are merely ritualistic (as above), serving no purpose and must be retracted at the right time. Others may need to be modified to stay relevant.

Organizational processes serve both Business and Technology equally, thus providing a unifying framework. But beyond this, their role in promoting BITA is somewhat indeterminate. However, many organizational processes, like IT security policy, recruitment process, software usage compliance policy, and procurement process depend on a robust alignment between Business and Technology to provide stability, consistency, continuance, and protection to the enterprise.

Exercise: List down all the internal processes in your company that you can think of. Classify these under functional and organizational. Against each process, mention "retain," "remove," or "modify" based on your view. For the modify category, cite the changes you seek. Get comparative views from your colleagues and peers to check if your views resonate with others.

By conducting this exercise over a wide enough cross-section, you may obtain a fair organizationwide recommendation on the desirable and undesirable organizational processes, which you may like to share with the owners of those processes for required action.

The new-generation workforce is not orientated toward too many controls and regulations, which they see as an attack on their liberty. If you have too many processes in the company, take it as a *red flag*. Organizational processes must be kept to the minimum number required. Fewer processes, like lower taxes, result in higher compliance.

Business Processes

Business processes are the collection of methods and procedures designed to serve the *customer* (or a primary external stakeholder—partner, regulator, etc.) of the enterprise. The essential thing about these processes is that they must be flexible and adaptable. Most companies start out with a brilliant set of processes, but many of these get overtaken in time by shifting customer expectations and experiences.

This is a vital point that sets the successful digital enterprises apart from the enterprises that are still struggling on the digital path. Almost all of us have had experiences with airlines, banks, hotels, telcos, and others that have left us perplexed and frustrated about the rationale behind the processes that are foisted on us as customers. Most often, the only explanation given is, "It's our company policy." End of discussion. It is a clear sign that the digital makeover of the enterprise is still nowhere close to completion.

On the other hand, some new Digital Age business processes like hailing a cab with Uber, or ordering merchandise with Amazon, are not only user-friendly and intuitive but also stay in lockstep with changes in the market environment and the rising expectations of their customers. This is not by chance. These companies have instituted advanced technologies, like sentiment analytics and data mining, to gauge customer experience parameters and respond to them even before they are expressed. And they have reaped a tidy benefit from this. Today, many digital enterprises owe their success almost entirely to sleek business processes that keep the customer squarely in the center.

Well-tuned business processes are among the best examples of BITA at work. Think of a merchandising firm that is into the delivery of sports goods from multiple vendors. The company has a convenient website that can be accessed on-the-go by anyone. A visitor to the site is encouraged to select a sport (say tennis) and then the gear that is required—say a tennis racquet. Next, it prompts the visitor to input their level, like a beginner, hobbyist, pro, and so on and recommends an array of matching products to choose from. At this point, you could also specify a make, type, or price range.

Once you have selected a product, you are guided either to choose more items (like tennis balls) or to a payment gateway. After verifying the payment, the order is confirmed and an order ID is issued to you. Then the process of order handling (invisible to you) takes over. For example, if the order consists of multiple items from different vendors, this must be decomposed and sent to each vendor in the chain, with the relevant order and shipment details. At each vendor's site, the dispatch and delivery process kicks in, which results in items getting shipped to you from different vendors. When you receive the shipments, an acknowledgment is sent by the deliverer to the front-end company, which then completes the order process and asks you to rate the experience! The flow is illustrated in Figure 4.2 in a very simplified and abridged form, the purpose being only to highlight that *multiple business processes*—each involving both Business and Technology working in harmony—are at work to execute a routine

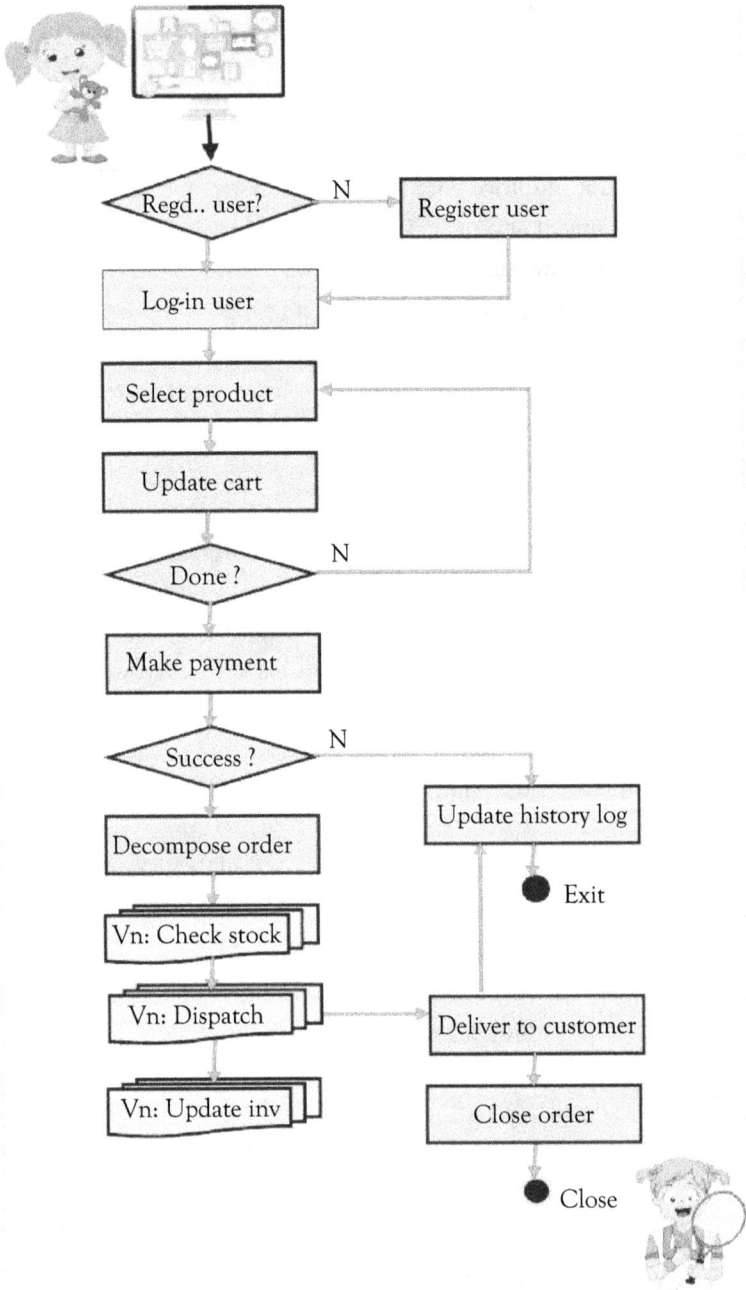

Figure 4.2 Simplified business process-flow example

customer request. Each box in the diagram is a detailed business process that could span multiple entities.

The simplicity and elegance of business applications are so fundamental to the customer experience in the digital age—from booking cinema tickets and taxis to banking and trading—that it has become the new normal. But at the end of the day, these are merely intuitive and innovative business processes at play, that were fashioned by using technology for creating business value. This is BITA at work.

Figure 4.3 depicts the general pattern of a business process delivery cycle, highlighting the importance of BITA in the conception, construction, and rendering of value-creating business services. Each business process, such as the boxes in the previous illustration, is an outcome of this cycle, which is a continuous one, running in sync with the customer lifecycle. Mining customer data and analyzing it for changes in behavior patterns, therefore, forms an integral part of the business process cycle.

Business and Technology work continuously and harmoniously throughout the business process cycle with the same vision and a shared sense of urgency to deliver and perfect the customer experience.

> **Exercise:** List down all the different Business processes running in your organization, that is, processes that have a direct or indirect bearing on the business outcome or customer experience in the left column of Table 4.1. Having done this, give your considered assessment on a 1–5 scale on the given set of attributes (see definitions following the table). It would be good to do this across several participants from Business and Technology.

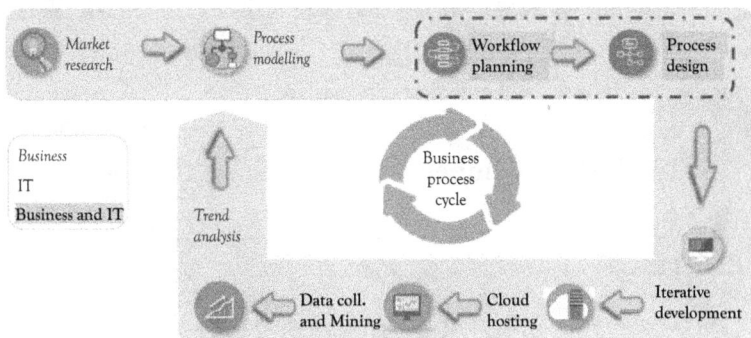

Figure 4.3 Business process cycle

Table 4.1 Process attributes

Business process	Conve- nience	Intuiti- veness	Flexi- bility	Simpli- city	Portabi- lity	Perfor- mance
---						

Convenience: If *you* were the customer (or user), would you consider that this process contributes to making things convenient for you?

Intuitiveness: Does the process anticipate needs and help the customer make more informed decisions? [Like time and price estimates, comparisons, alternatives, reviews, history, offers …]

Flexibility: What is the level of openness to changes in the process? How easy is it to personalize the process for specific markets or segments?

Simplicity: Would your parents, or other people of an older generation, be comfortable using this process without assistance?

Portability: How accommodative is the process in adapting to different environments? [multiple devices, cloud, operating systems, future trends]

Performance: How well does the process work under varying load and traffic conditions, on parameters such as the speed of response and stability?

When averaged over multiple respondents, this could become a simple yet effective tool for gauging business process effectiveness in meeting the customer benchmark on critical parameters, and for focusing attention on the relative shortcomings. You could go a step further with this— create a checklist of 10 or more items against *each* parameter (e.g., 10 factors contributing to *convenience*) and ask people to rate the process on every one of them. The results will greatly supplement your efforts to win your customers' goodwill and stay competitive.

Instinctual Connect—the ICing on the cake

Example 4.3

I was at one of those frequent offsite meetings that span a weekend. The only difference here was that it happened to be my wife's birthday that

> *weekend. I did the only possible thing that could rescue me from a sticky aftermath. I placed an online order early in the morning for delivering flowers to her. It required me to select a bouquet online, fill the details, and make the payment.*
>
> *I reached home the next day. My wife showed me the flowers that she had got from me, which were now placed in a vase in our sitting room. She also showed me the card which had accompanied the flowers. Apart from the usual Happy Birthday, there was a line saying, "wish I could be there in person." Now, this was surprising, because I had missed giving such an instruction, assuming it would be rather self-evident anyway! But when I did see it, I was glad for this simple message. It was probably the reason that there was less strain on my arrival than I was anticipating. A happy ending after all!*

In this example, the addition of those simple words was an improvisation, arising from an understanding of the customer's situation. The prescribed process was not bypassed at any point, but an intuitive gesture lent further fizz to a predictable and comparatively lackluster outcome. Maybe the flower shop had picked this up from long experience, or it was an impromptu act of someone dispatching the order. I am not sure. But who do you think I would go to for my next online flower shopping, or if asked to recommend a flower delivery service? You guessed it. And why? Because of the *instinctual connect.* Had it been as per the prescribed process, I may not have complained, but would probably also not have remembered the transaction and write about it years later.

In case of a process, the defined steps—which are usually documented—are fixed and unchanging. This makes processes very amenable to automation. An instinctual connect, on the other hand, while sharing the same goal as a process, is a *variable human action* that is neither documented nor templatized. In other words, it is *improvisation*, which is done to make the process outcome more dazzling.

Quantum physics tells us about the uncertainty principle, postulated by Heisenberg. Its core premise is that there is a degree of unpredictability even in the ordered universe, otherwise governed by the precise laws of science. But for this, everything—including our behaviors—would be entirely predictable. How dull would that be! It is the same with processes. Without instinctual connect, process outcomes would be dreary and predictable, with almost no room to enthrall its (human) participants. It is the instinctual connect that stimulates a process to achieve more than its potential, and hence, this forms a vital *tool for differentiation* in a business setting.

To enhance your customers' experience at all stages of the lifecycle, an instinctual connect between Business and Technology is, therefore, a prerequisite in this era of digitally driven business.

An instinctual connect is situational and intuitive. A close alignment between Business and Technology drives proactive behavior leading to instinctual connect between the people, which further strengthens alignment. When such a continuous cycle is set in motion, the teams displays all the core human qualities and values mentioned in Figure 4.4, leading to behaviors (and outcomes) that no structured process or automation can produce.

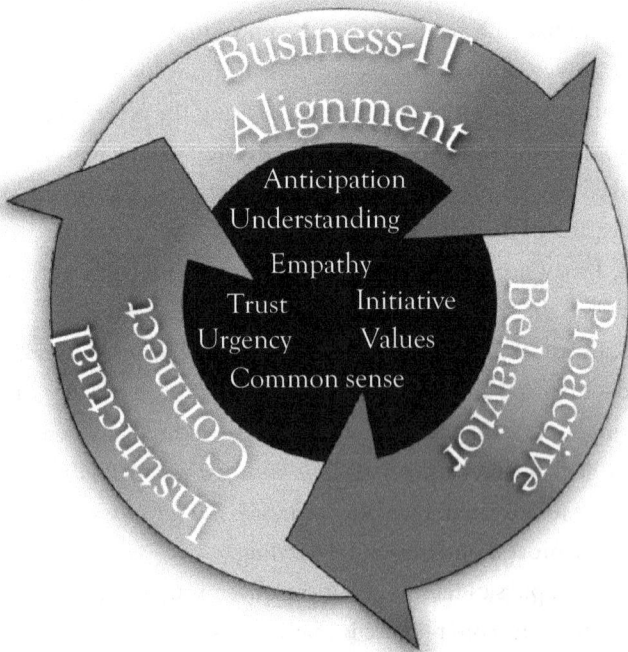

Figure 4.4 Instinctual connect

> **Exercise:** *Reflect on the Instinctual Connect examples in your own company. List down cases that you were part of (or are aware of) where Instinctual Connect between Business and IT helped in making the outcome of a business process more rewarding. What are the factors that were (or can be) responsible for building up to this level of alignment?*

Tools and Technology

In a modern enterprise environment, there is an abundance of tools and technology to accomplish business objectives. Tools boost performance by enabling higher productivity, faster transactions, accurate and timely availability of actionable information, drilled down analytics, and a host of other value additions. Today, almost every industry segment relies on software tools for its core operations. Though diverse in their core focus, these segments have a common denominator in the adoption of automated tools for their internal (e.g., ERP) and external (e.g., CRM) operations to propel their growth. In a typical scenario, it is these *tools* that fit together as the *building blocks* of the enterprise's business process workflow, glued together by Instinctual Connect.

Using software tools and technology, either as individual productivity boosters or as enterprise process enablers, serves another very important purpose: It *brings Business and Technology together* to create a new ecosystem of empowerment and information, better suited to meet the demands of digital markets. BITA gets a boost when technology and tools are well-absorbed across the breadth and depth of the organization.

However, even in these times, there are numerous adoption challenges associated with new technology, commonly due to ignorance and inertia, or simply tight comfort zones that some people are unwilling to renounce. Everyone is not tech-savvy, nor a fan of technology. It requires a well-focused approach led by top management to sell the value of productivity and business enhancing tools, as a cultural shift. Employees must be convinced of the impact and benefits of the tools—at Business and individual level. Adoption of new technologies in the enterprise environment must itself be a dedicated process, built around some proven practices such as the following:

1.   Presenting a simple user interface.
2.   Customizing your coaching.
3.   Enthusing the leaders first.
4.   Propagating the success stories.
5.   Saluting the pioneers.
6.   Dis-incentivizing the stragglers.
7.   Building and nurturing champions.

As a running, or even aspiring digital enterprise, you must invest not just in creating elegant processes for Business and Technology, but in their *fusion*. This is accomplished by enabling the sharing of information across processes, using an enterprise system bus. This seamless sharing is accomplished using enterprise application integration (EAI) techniques, the details of which are not relevant here. Conceptually, this is like the system bus in a computer system—a single bus that connects the major components of a computer system to achieve their harmonious interplay (Figure 4.5).

Efforts made to align at the level of functional, organizational, and business process, topped by an instinctual connect between Business and Technology indeed go a long way in strengthening BITA at the process dimension. There are, however, some other important aspects, often ignored in our fixation with the urgent, which would bear upon making your BITA more comprehensive and enduring.

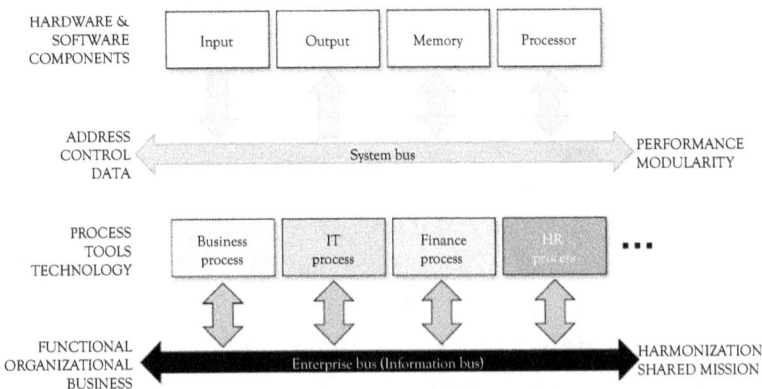

Figure 4.5 Sharing of information across processes—enterprise bus

Continuous Improvement

When we follow a process multiple times, we subconsciously get better at it. However, for alignment, continuous improvement must be pursued in a *systematic and planned* way by both Business and Technology. This usually happens by setting incremental goals that are jointly pursued by Business and Technology. For example, leveraging Big data for continually increasing the level of detail and sophistication in gathering actionable insights on customer behavior. With progressive customer expectations, continuous improvement is your ticket to staying ahead in the game. Never stop asking the question, "How can we do this better?" with the conviction that there's always a way!

Continuous improvement does not mean that instead of focusing on what is new, we just refine the old. While the electric light did not come from the continuous improvement of candles, the 787 Dreamliner was a result of constant improvement of the Boeing 247 (1933). The point here is that excellence is a function of both out-box-thinking *and* continuous improvement. One does not *substitute* the other.

Notice that the business process cycle (Figure 4.3) has continuous feedback on customer behavior, in addition to input from external market research, which is used to refine the process continually—to make things better for the customer. A break in this cycle would signal a failure of BITA and blunt the competitive edge. *Any* process flow that misses the feedback loop calls for a *red flag*.

Even right now, there may be several processes in your company that are crying for improvement. Can you single some of these out? List what it would take to tune them to the stakeholders' expectations.

Change Management

An essential requisite of BITA is the management of change by Business and Technology in a shared and disciplined manner.

A disciplined approach to managing change requires a constant emphasis on various stages of the cycle, as shown in Figure 4.6, and tracking the changes using advanced tools. If your organization does not have a formal, organizationwide change management process that governs your

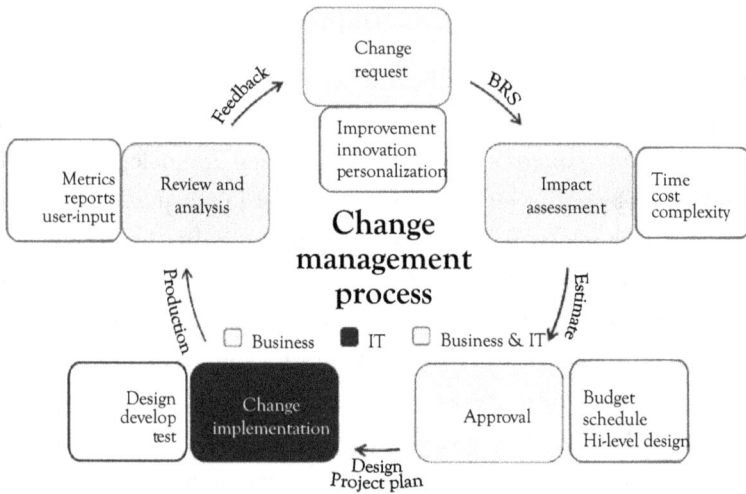

Figure 4.6 Change management process

products, procedures, practices, and policies, it is only a matter of time before it is struck down by market forces, which are increasingly dynamic.

Managing change goes far beyond implementing advanced tools. The need for the change must be clearly understood by both Business and Technology, as a calling that impels them to respond to it with a shared sense of urgency. It often helps to appoint *change champions* from Business and Technology to rally the forces. Think through the obstacles that may hinder the path of change implementation and make efforts to remove them *before* they puncture the wheel. Go for some quick wins to switch the dissenters over with the results. With time, things settle down as the changes mature and are mainstreamed. But by then, it is time for the next change!

Quality

Ever wonder why the term quality does not mesmerize us anymore? We gloss over the term in campaigns and ads. Isn't it important now? Well, it sure is, but in this age, quality is no longer a *differentiator*. It is *hygiene*. In other words, you are *expected* to maintain certain standards of quality and, therefore, trumpeting it fails to impress. While accomplishing your quality goals might not guarantee your place in the market, *not* accomplishing them is undoubtedly the quickest way to exit the market. Today, customers do not *expect* defects in the product or the service, so trying to impress by fixing them quickly will achieve nothing. Quality is a proactive, not a reactive indicator.

While quality is a given, the tricky part is achieving it at a reasonable *cost*. It is imperative that Business and Technology understand the implications of delayed discovery of flaws or defects. The earlier a defect is caught, the less it costs to fix. A defect that escapes through all the stages of quality assurance (testing) and is first found by the *customer* is the worst kind. Such "escaping" defects are the costliest to fix both from a monetary and goodwill standpoint. One of the damaging fallouts of the disconnect between Business and Technology is the invisibility of the spiraling cost of quality, which could manifest in severe margin erosion. BITA is your best bet against such an eventuality.

When you buy your next car, who would you prefer to test drive it? I'm sure you'll like to do this yourself, rather than tell the manufacturer to do it. Yet, when it comes to testing new business applications, many organizations let Technology (IT), which "manufactured" the artifact, do the *user* acceptance testing. Unless the *Business* organization does the final testing, the product cannot be considered tested.

In summary, quality results from an inborn passion for excellence shared by Business and Technology teams in spirit and action. On this journey without an end, shortcuts don't exist.

In conclusion, enterprise processes are needed to bring some method to the pandemonium in the business environment. We spoke of processes in terms of *functional*, *organizational*, and *business* clusters, each of which influences BITA in its own way. The *Instinctual Connect* was introduced as an icing on the process pie and an essential element in the enhancement of BITA and customer experience.

CHAPTER 5

The Intellectual Interlock

"Time may not be on your side, but innovation is."

History has recorded many famous predictions by eminent people, from almost every sphere of human endeavor, which testify to the transcendent nature of the human spirit. Not because these predictions were *accurate*—in fact, they were anything *but*—but because *of their failure to daunt the future generations from breaking the barriers* that they imposed. Here are some specimens from diverse fields.

Computers and communications:

"There is no reason anyone would want a computer in their home." Ken Olson, President, Chairman, and Founder of the Digital Equipment Corporation (1977).

"There is practically no chance that communication space satellites will be used to provide better telephone, telegraph, television, or radio service inside the United States." T Craven, FCC Chief (1961).

"The Internet will soon go spectacularly supernova and in 1996 catastrophically collapse." Robert Metcalfe, the inventor of the Ethernet (1995).

Atomic energy:
"A rocket will never be able to leave the Earth's atmosphere." Headline of an article published in *the New York Times* based on a collective view of the advanced scientific community (1936).

"There is not the slightest indication that nuclear energy will ever be obtainable. It would mean that the atom would have to be shattered at will." *Albert Einstein* (1932).

"The energy produced by the breaking down of the atom is a very poor kind of thing. Anyone who expects a source of power from the

---

transformation of these atoms is talking moonshine." Ernest Ruther-ford, known as the father of nuclear physics (1933).

Aviation:

"There will never be a bigger plane built." Boeing chief engineer, after the first flight of the Boeing 247–a twin-engine plane that could hold 10 people (1933).

"Heavier-than-air flying machines are impossible." Lord Kelvin, British mathematician and physicist.

Entertainment:

"The cinema is a little more than a fad. It's canned drama. What audiences really want is flesh and blood on the stage." Charlie Chaplin, celebrated comic-actor, film-maker, and composer.

"Television will not be able to hold on to any market it captures after the first six months. People will soon get tired of staring at a plywood box every night." Darryl Zanuck, famous film producer.

Military:

"I must confess that my imagination refuses to see any sort of submarine doing anything but suffocating its crew and floundering at sea." H. G. Wells, British sci-fi writer (1901)

"The idea that the cavalry will be replaced by these iron coaches is absurd. It is little short of treasonous." The *aide-de-camp to Field Marshall Haig*, while witnessing a tank demonstration (1916).

The above examples attest the fact that the only limitations we have are the ones we place on ourselves. Imagine where we would have been as a society if all "educated" prophecies about the future had remained unchallenged. Thankfully, the passion for questioning set limits prevailed, and our course on the waves of time was recharted. Think about it. If Einstein had not questioned the famed Newton's law of gravitation, general relativity—one of the towering achievements of twentieth-century physics, and the basis of our present understanding of the universe—would never have been postulated. Examples like these are everywhere, each hiding countless setbacks, ridicules, and frustrations behind that one eureka moment.

The question is, what's next? Light-speed travel, brain–computer interface (BCI), teleportation, immortality, interstellar travel, or colonization of exoplanets? So many possibilities and all considered beyond human scope currently. Indeed, the ramifications are so astounding as to seem utterly unbelievable. Take BCI as an example. It potentially implies that a pair of high-resolution cameras can be interfaced directly with your brain to function as your eyes, and other mechanical devices to function as your limbs. Now, a computer interface, unlike the nervous system, is not limited by proximity and can extend over vast distances. This implies that while you (defined as your brain) are in location X, your eyes and arms, can extend to locations Y and Z, still controlled by your brain (Figure 5.1). X, Y, and Z can be on different continents, communicating via satellites in space! In other words, a single human can be all over the globe at the same time. It is hard even to imagine the implications of this on our civilization.

The goal here is to convey the importance of creative thought and *innovation*, the subject of this chapter, in human evolution by stressing that there is no dream too large, no fantasy unimaginable, and no frontiers beyond our reach. Fear of failure, not lack of imagination, is the biggest impediment to innovation.

The terms innovation and creativity are often used interchangeably. Both pertain to ingenuity and are functions of the intellect. It is common to refer to originality in the *artistic* pursuits as *creative*, and in *scientific*

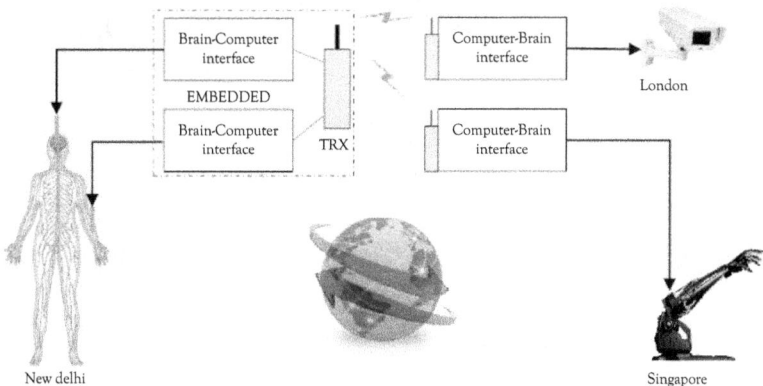

Figure 5.1 Brain–computer interface

and *technological* matters as *innovative*. In the context of a business enterprise, both creativity and innovation are relevant, but there are subtle differences.

Creativity is about *imagining* new things. Innovation is about *doing* new things. Creativity refers to ideas. Innovation refers to making ideas happen. A creative idea becomes an innovation when it leads to a product, process, or practice that is (a) desirable, (b) feasible, (c) viable, and (d) doable (Figure 5.2). If an idea does not meet all these criteria, it may still be a *creative* one, though not necessarily *innovative*.

Innovation has a lot to do with breaking the confines of established practices and daring to be different. Hence the term *out*-of-the-box. Enterprises centered on *replicating* others—employing similar people, doing similar things, producing similar products, but expecting to somehow achieve superior results—do not become market leaders.

Being open to ideas, even from the relatively inexperienced, is the essence of an *innovation-driven culture*, especially in this era, when being different is so central to business success.

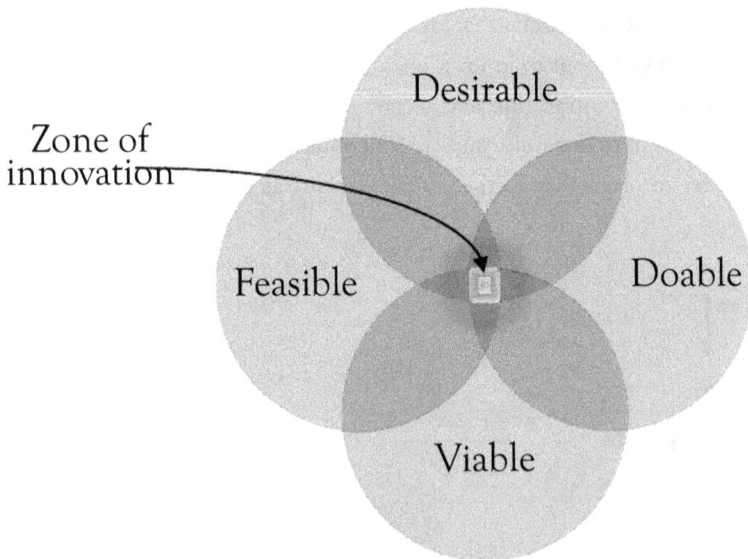

Figure 5.2 Zone of innovation

Example 5.1

A mobile telecom company was on an expansion mode to increase the network coverage and capacity in its country of operation. Obviously, for increased capacity and coverage, you needed to buy more equipment from the network equipment provider (NEP), which was an expensive proposition. Given the fiercely competitive nature of the market and wafer-thin margins, any savings here went a long way in strengthening the bottom-lines. The challenge was to increase capacity and coverage by a factor of X, but cost by a fraction of X. Like the very eminent folks in the examples at the start of this chapter, the Chief Technology Officer of this company said, "this is impossible. More capacity requires more equipment and hence a proportionally higher cost."

*The teams were asked to deliberate it further and come back with a proposal to the management. The Technology and Business folks got together to try and find an out-of-the-box solution. One of the participants here was a young business-finance manager (BFM), who raised his hand hesitatingly to ask for permission to suggest. He proposed that instead of buying equipment from the NEP, the company should lease capacity from the NEP and pay for it as a **service**, based on the traffic carried by the NEP's network in a given period (say, every month), instead of a lump-sum for the quantity of equipment deployed. This, he continued, would motivate the NEP to optimize the equipment required for a given capacity, while sharing the operating company's mission of improved network traffic (and revenues). The operating company need not own the equipment and associated overheads, just run the services, perhaps achieving efficiency gains. He went on to say that he got this idea from the freight-wagon model, wherein one doesn't **buy** wagons, just lease capacity depending on load. It was indeed a breakthrough idea and after some discussion was unanimously adopted. The management loved it, and the model was weaved into the RFP. Of course, the NEPs were a bit uncomfortable initially, but as it translated into sound recurring revenues, joined in enthusiastically later. The "Capacity-as-a-Service" model became hugely successful and became the basis of all future contracts.*

INVENTION
RL Stevenson

INNOVATION

Figure 5.3 Invention and innovation

This is not an isolated example. The *digital enterprise* model, which includes the *aggregation* of goods and services (from multiple partners) through a simple user interface, is another excellent example of *established* methods being challenged to bring better, faster, and cheaper goods and services to millions of consumers across the globe.

The above example also demonstrates the power of *collaboration* in generating innovative solutions. When we are *within* an established system, we become part of it. Inertia chokes innovation. It often takes someone from *outside* to unlock the door to new possibilities. Thus, stay receptive. You never know where your next break-through idea is coming from.

Innovation is also sometimes considered synonymous with invention, but there's a difference (Figure 5.3). Invention is the *seed* that flowers into innovation. In other words, innovation is the practical consequence of an invention. Invention is often attributable to a single idea or a person behind it, whereas innovation is its continuous evolution over time by multiple ideas and persons. An invention has a culmination—a single eureka moment. Innovation is an ongoing process.

> **Exercise:** *Can you list at least five things that your company is doing which no one in your industry is doing? It could be products, practices, or processes. How are these contributing to your business results?*

Innovation in the Digital Age

Today's digital revolution is a consequence of enterprises embracing innovation. If there is one feature that distinguishes the Digital Age from its predecessors—most notably the industrial age and the distribution age—it is the mainstreaming of innovation, or the challenging of established systems, in the formal and informal course of business.

> *FedEx started life as a document delivery service. Its success was largely owed to its impeccable track record of guaranteed overnight delivery of documents to businesses and individuals in the continental United States, making them the undisputed leaders in this in-demand segment. So, when some disruptive digital innovations—like World Wide Web, low-cost scanners, and PDFs—arrived on the scene, which enabled people to simply e-mail documents to anyone across the globe in a jiffy, did it sound the death knell for FedEx? Far from it. Instead of being threatened by these powerful forces, or trying somehow to compete with and beat them, it reinvented itself and became the leading supply chain and logistics company, emerging as the backbone of e-commerce by embracing the very technologies that threatened its survival. From being a delivery company that took advantage of technology, it became a technology company that took advantage of delivery.[5]*

This example captures the essence of an innovation-driven enterprise environment, which is a precondition for business leadership in the Digital Age.

An enterprise's culture is said to be innovation-driven when its people regularly display all the attributes in Table 5.1. Not *only* imagination and ingenuity. It would be brazen to expect that everyone in the enterprise would be creative, curious, competent, committed, compatible, courageous, and confident. However, every successful enterprise has a clutch of

Table 5.1 Innovation attributes

What it takes (Innovation requires...)	Who it takes (A person who is...)
Imagination and ingenuity	Creative
Constantly questioning the conventional	Curious
Understanding of technology	Competent
Drive and passion	Committed
Embracing Change	Compatible
Taking risks	Courageous
Overcoming fear of failure	Confident

such people, who are its backbone. Given the right climate, invigorated by collaboration and alignment, these qualities can be *cultivated*. For example, a recognition system based on "dare-to-try" goes a long way in imparting confidence and courage to competent people to set free creative ideas.

Innovation has been the subject of in-depth study and many scholarly articles. Our intent here is not to research it but to understand how BITA can be used to leverage it in this Digital Age. To keep our discussion

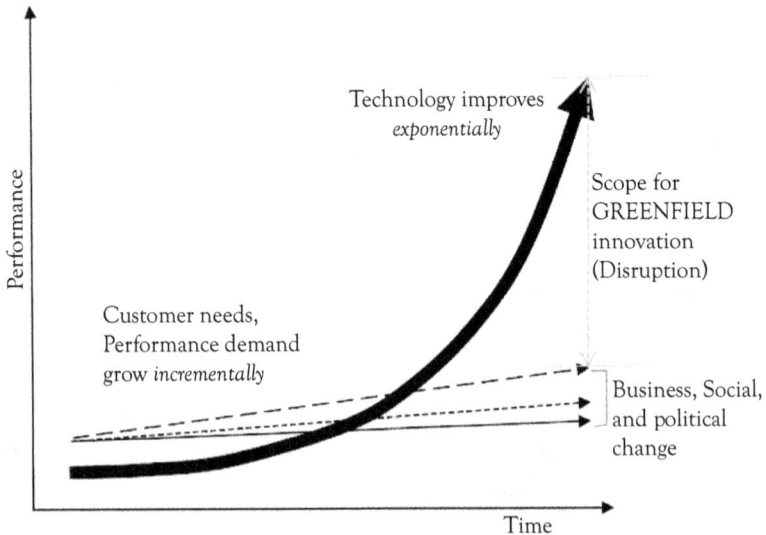

Figure 5.4 Disruptive innovation

simple and focused, let us tag innovation in two separate buckets. We will term the innovation in the first bucket as *greenfield*, and the innovation in the second bucket as *garden variety*. (These are arbitrary labels, don't Google them.) All breakthrough innovation—the Internet, the Maglev (Shanghai), Cloud Technology, Jet-propulsion, 3D Printing, and Driverless cars—is of the *greenfield* type, because it is *disruptive*, suddenly emerging as a towering edifice on a vacant, desolate expanse of green turf. Greenfield innovation happens when the pace of technology dramatically overtakes the pace of social, political, and business change (Figure 5.4). The thing about Greenfield innovation is that you never know when the next one is going to happen. Greenfield innovations don't happen every day, but when they do, they shake things up a bit.

Our area of interest here is the more common, but subtler, garden-variety innovation. This is not dependent on the next big thing in science, technology, or economics but on the application of thought to everyday matters. The essence of garden-variety innovation is the questioning spirit

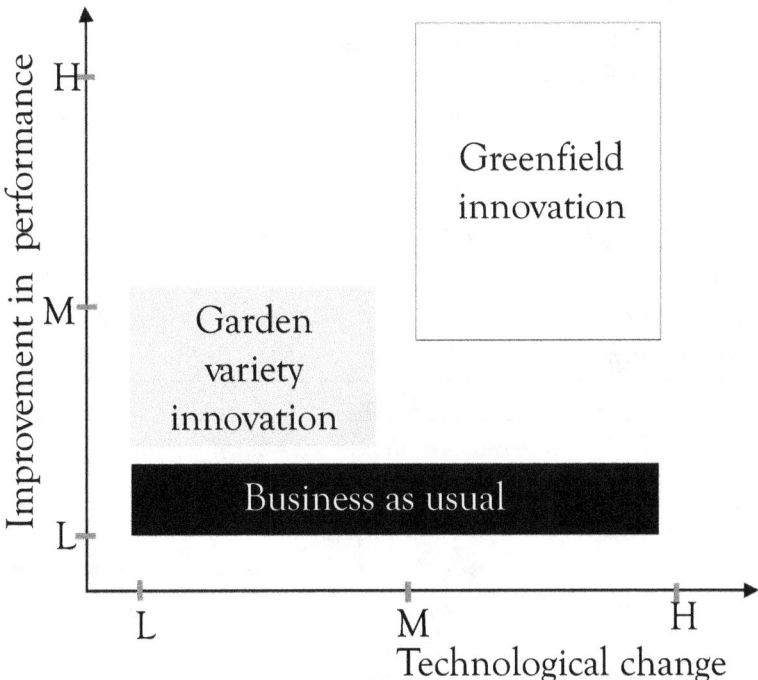

Figure 5.5 Greenfield and garden-variety innovation

and out-of-box thinking applied to familiar subjects for achieving incremental improvements. Much of the garden-variety innovation comes not from scientists and experts, but from regular students, employees, business folks, consumers—people like you and me. Sliced bread and the self-heating butter knife are two good examples of garden-variety innovation. The simple but intuitive user-interfaces on many mobile apps are others. Unless specified otherwise, the term "innovation" here will henceforth refer to *garden variety* innovation (Figure 5.4).

Innovation can be used to find ways around complex business problems or to gain a competitive edge through differentiation. We commonly encounter examples of garden-variety innovation in every walk of life, often driven by BITA. Can you site a few examples from your experiences with various businesses like banks, shops, airlines, and so on?

> *Competition in the mobile telecom space in India had intensified due to the entry of new operators and ensuing price wars. Customer retention was becoming a challenge, even as tariffs kept dropping. At such a time, the companies with better alignment between their Business and Technology arms could quickly launch some innovative plans and gain a first mover advantage. These innovations included per second charging (fair usage pricing), dynamic tariff plans based on airtime demand in an area, personalized offers allowing the subscriber to create their own plans, and so on. The telcos with innovative offerings had much higher churn-in than their price-slashing peers. In the longer run, these were the operators that have survived, not the price droppers.*

> *Getting feedback from customers during check-out is a common practice with reputed hotels. However, when you see real action on the ground based on these inputs, it is a pleasant surprise. Many times, the solution to customer grievances is not quite straightforward. That's when you need to dial into innovation. A hotel that I once checked into gave excellent evidence of this. It had received numerous complaints about long check-in queues at the reception desk and how it caused frustration to even its most*

> *loyal customers. The management debated this and came up with a plan. They invited the Technology team and worked with them to launch a simple mobile app for self-check-in. Confirmed customers could simply walk up to kiosks in the reception area, which would spew out a card key when fed with the confirmation code generated by the mobile app, saving not only queue time for guests but also freeing up the hassled front-desk personnel to engage in more customer-experience-enhancing tasks. I am sure the thinking was that if airlines can do it, what's stopping hotels? Cross-industry pollination of ideas often works wonders for the business.*

Much of the innovation in business happens to meet *un*stated customer requirements. Being first in the market, even with an *incremental* offering may provide a substantial competitive edge. Companies, which recognize that o*nly the constant pursuit of innovation can ensure long-term success*, thus have a significant advantage over their larger and better-entrenched peers who value convention over transformation.

> ***Exercise:*** *Think back. Can you come up with an innovation in your industry—say by your competition—that you found very appealing? Would the same have been encouraged and adopted by your own company? If not, what are the factors that have prevented it? How can they be overcome?*

Igniting Innovation with BITA

While most of us do not need convincing about the edge that innovation brings, we are not always clear on how to unlock the potential for innovation within.

To answer this, we need to understand garden-variety innovation more fully in the context of modern business. First, it is not the preserve of a select few. Second, it is not a thought or a brainwave. It is *action* aimed at making ideas happen. Third, it is most often the result of several minds working in *unison*, guided by a shared vision. And fourth, it does not end with one idea or action. It is a *continuous* process that combines a multitude of incremental ideas (and actions) from diverse sources in a harmonious way for constant value addition. These properties are central to building the conditions for innovation to thrive in the enterprise.

Inculcating these in your organizational philosophy, attitudes, habits, and practices is therefore crucial to creating the environment in which innovation blooms.

Though these appear to be rather obvious and uncomplicated, many enterprises are found to lean more toward the properties on the *right* (in Figure 5.6). That is, innovation is the preserve of *just a select few* (whose voice is heard), defined by *ideas alone* (not followed through), achieved by *acting in isolation* (in a silo structure), and happens *exceptionally* (matter of chance).

There are techniques available to tap into the innovation potential that is latent in people and organizations. You may have picked up some of these through experience and by participating in focused innovation workshops like The Six Thinking Hats[6] and Lateral Thinking[7] (De Bono). These provide some excellent tools and insights that can be applied to *leverage BITA for innovation.*

Specific situations may call for different techniques to be employed for distilling the innovation potential of a group, but all these techniques have the above four properties inherent in them, as we shall see. BITA brings in the required diversity of thought and action to leverage this potential fully for enterprise success. In other words, organizations with a strong BITA are much better equipped to tap into the inherent potential for innovation by leveraging all its essential properties.

We discussed earlier in this chapter about the inherent personal traits (creativity, curiosity, courage, etc.) that are desired in the workforce for stimulating the innovative streak. These personal traits, amplified by spirited participation of *both* Business and Technology, form the backdrop of the discussion that follows on the different techniques of stimulating innovation.

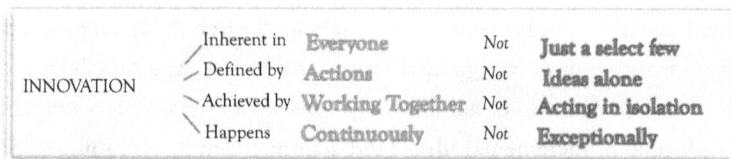

	Inherent in	Everyone	Not	**Just a select few**
INNOVATION	Defined by	Actions	Not	**Ideas alone**
	Achieved by	Working Together	Not	**Acting in isolation**
	Happens	Continuously	Not	**Exceptionally**

Figure 5.6 *Garden-variety innovation characteristics*

Brainstorming

Perhaps the most common practice in office environments the world over, *brainstorming* is a powerful problem-solving technique. The primary focus here is to get many minds focused on a single problem simultaneously.

To get the best from brainstorming, you must ensure the following:

1. *No domination.* Typically, brainstorming sessions with the CEO or other senior folks don't go very well. People are generally uncomfortable about speaking up, and free flow of ideas does not happen, defeating the very purpose of brainstorming. Brainstorming works best in an uninhibited environment, typically among peers.
2. *No evaluation.* The woods would be very silent if only those birds sang that sang the best. Same goes for ideas during brainstorming. No idea is too trivial to be ignored. Speak up without fear.
3. *Moderation.* Moderation is required to ensure that everyone gets a chance to put forth their ideas. The moderator may choose a round-robin method, or any other, to ensure that every voice is heard and recorded.
4. *Follow-up.* Nothing frustrates people more than their ideas going into cold storage. Brainstorming is not an end, but the beginning of an extensive process, whose progress and outcome must be visible to all participants.

Example 5.2

I was engaged as a consultant by a management consultancy firm ("CF") to help CF add its in-house IT strength as a portfolio element in its basket of offerings to clients, rather than just keeping the internal IT systems humming. The nature of this engagement was highly confidential and strictly time-bound, and frankly, I was a bit unsure about how exactly to help CF in my interim capacity. It would take me weeks of research to determine and prioritize the exact issues. Luckily, brainstorming came to my rescue making my task infinitely easier.

> *On my very first day, I asked for a late-evening meeting with all available Business folks and a few senior people from IT. I wrote a simple question on the board: "What is preventing the transformation of IT from an internally-focused entity to a customer-value creator?" Many new and unexpected answers came up. We combined similar statements to create a final list of some ten "real" inhibitors. I then asked the team question number 2: "Which of these must be tackled right now in the best interest of CF's clients?" There was some debate on this, but we finally reached a list of four problems that the team agreed required immediate attention.*
>
> *The next morning, I gathered AF's IT team members and chalked down the four inhibitors as a problem statement. I then posed my third question: "What must we do to overcome these?" After an initial train of the usual suspects, we generated some innovative and out-of-box solutions. The team conceded that they had never got together as a group to think through these problems. But once they did, there was an amazing flow of ideas, backed by a strong and unanimous commitment to deliver. I felt that 70 percent of my work was done! The plan was quickly accepted by the management and we were assured of their deep and continuous involvement throughout the implementation. All it had taken to get started on the right path was a couple of serious brainstorming sessions.*

A slight variation of the brainstorming technique is the *brain writing* process, where ideas, instead of being spoken aloud, are submitted as written statements, pasted on a board, and collated.

Bucketization

This is a simple technique for organizing the thinking process. It entails breaking down the subject into smaller and smaller units, or buckets, for generating more numerous and contextual ideas. The following simple example will make this clearer and help you apply this in practice.

Everyone who has ever appeared for a job interview is familiar with this most common poser: *Tell us about yourself.* How do you go about this? Well, here is one possible response.

*I am a senior associate with D&X Consulting, which I joined three years ago. I am very fond of traveling, especially to places that are rich in natural beauty, like mountains and forests. I graduated in computer science near the top of my class three years ago and was among the first to be picked up on campus. I received my last promotion just six months ago, and all my performance ratings have been in the top bracket. I love socializing and am quick to make friends. My company sent me overseas to Europe to work onsite with a client a year ago, and it was an experience of tremendous value, both for my cultural exposure and professional standing. I hail from a small town in eastern India where I did my schooling in vernacular medium but cleared the competition to get into a top university for graduation in computer science. Cricket has been my passion since early childhood, though I couldn't play at a professional level, which is a lasting regret. I am proficient in C++ and have also completed PMI certification successfully. When I was fourteen, I was selected to represent my school in an interschool debating competition, where I spoke against deforestation. I won that debate. In the long run, about 10 years from now, I would like to become an entrepreneur using my inborn business acumen and acquired professional experience. By temperament, I am a curious person who likes to try out new things, as I did in the science lab at my college—sometimes with disastrous results! I am also very tech-savvy, and my friends come up to me for help with the latest smart devices…
(and so on).*

Seems to be a nice enough guy, but there's a problem in the response. To most interviewers, this would blur the view and hence would take away a great deal from his prospects. And the problem is, the response is not *organized*, randomly jumping from one theme to another. Such a response could be prone to *gaps* and give evidence of a clouded and cluttered mind. A clear thought process would look at breaking up the response into distinct topics, each of which is *individually thought through* before moving on. In the above case, it would be a lot more career-enhancing for the candidate if he were to *organize* his response into topical buckets, as shown in Figure 5.7.

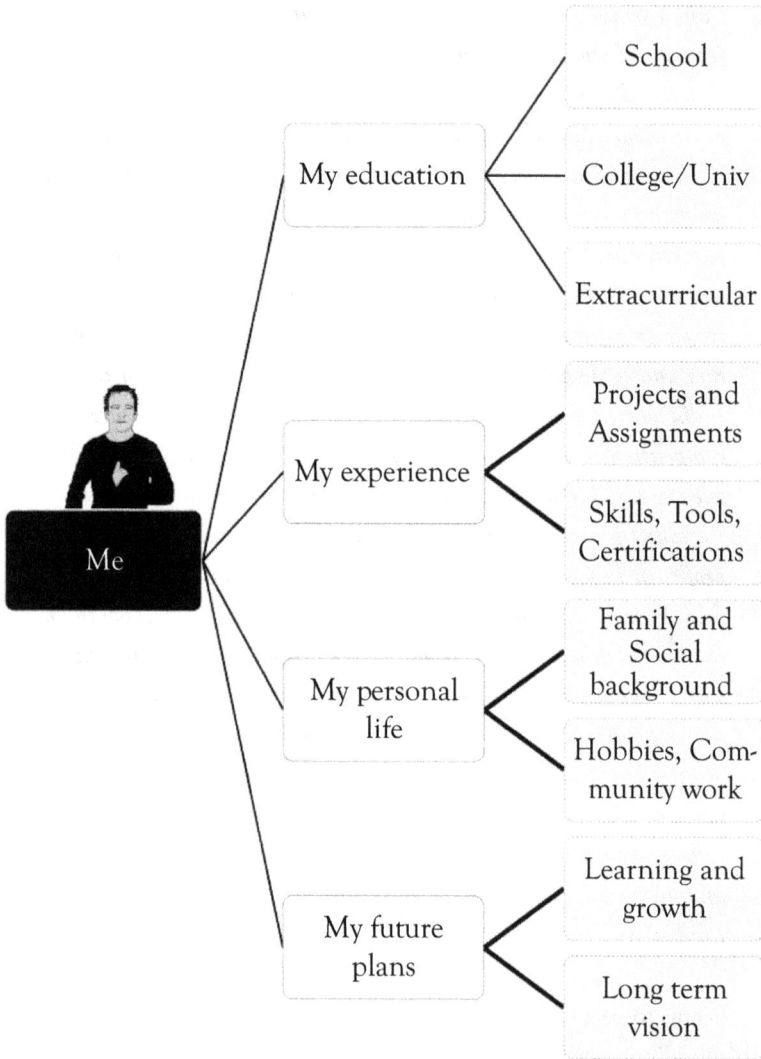

Figure 5.7 Organizing thought-process through bucketization

This process is called bucketizing because it entails organizing the ideas into successively smaller containers (buckets). There are large buckets (like education in our example), within which there are smaller buckets (like college). There can be many bucket levels, bringing more granularity to the ideation process. You may decide the order in which you wish to go, but the important thing is that while you are concentrating on one bucket, you must resist the temptation to jump to a different bucket.

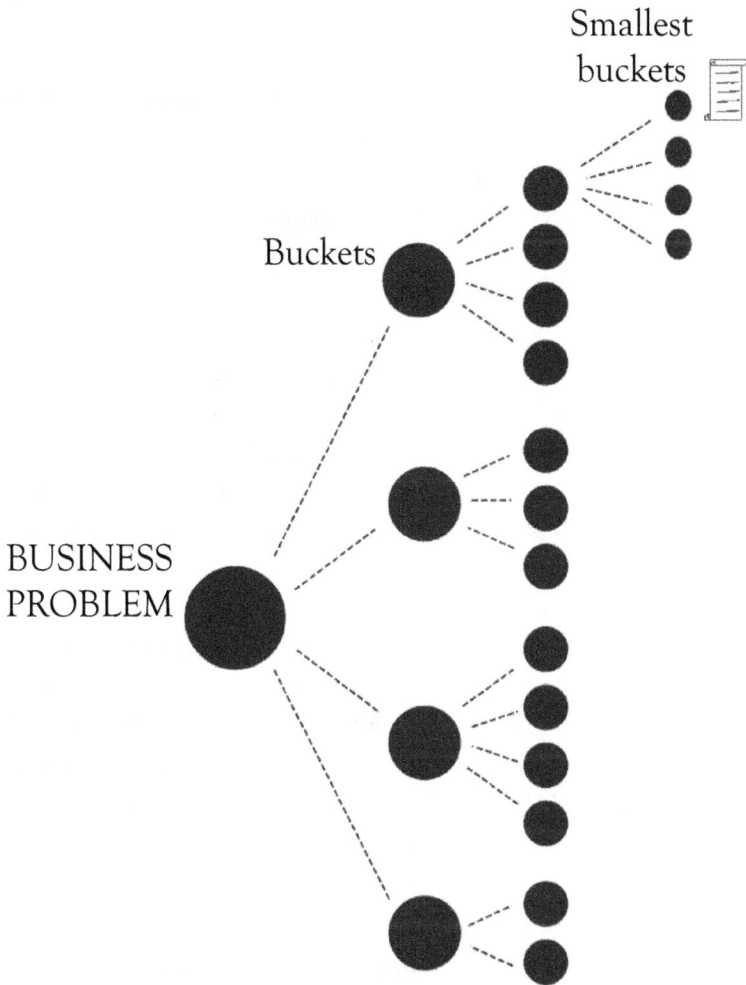

Figure 5.8 Organizing ideas through bucketization technique

Bucketizing helps generate more numerous ideas around a topic (Figure 5.8). Applying this technique in business situations is a simple but very effective way of drilling deep and coming up with hidden gems. It is done best in a group setting with participation from Business and Technology folks. Take any business issue, like how to enhance the customers' experience, or how to run the project on cost and schedule, or deciding the features of a new product, and apply bucketizing to break the larger theme into successively smaller buckets. Start filling the *smallest* buckets with ideas. In the end, you will have a generous compilation of ideas in each of the smallest buckets, making up a well-ordered collection.

Contrast this with randomly trying to list down ideas, following no structure in the ideation process. *Bucketizing is a great way to set-free those brilliant ideas that you didn't even know were locked in your brain.* At every step, ask this question: "What *other* possibilities exist to break this down?"

Fusion

There is no province where the power of *intersection* as a multiplier of value is more forcefully apparent than in stimulation of innovative thinking.

Fusion is a by-product of intersection. It is the ability of ideas in one realm to fuse, or blend, with ideas in a *different* realm, spawning innovative concepts. It's a form of *cross-fertilization* of ideas, germinating new possibilities.

> *The traditional mercury-based blood-pressure monitoring system had been in use by doctors for decades. Then it emerged, probably during a conversation between medical experts and electronics buffs, that the vibrations in the arterial wall caused by the inflation and deflation of the cuff around the upper arm could be sensed by a transducer and converted into electrical signals that could produce a digital readout. And thus was born the digital BP monitor, now part of everyone's medical repertoire at home (I am not sure how many homes ever kept those mercury-based contraptions at hand). Had only electronics engineers, or only doctors, however brilliant in their respective fields, worked on this in isolation, I doubt if such a device would have evolved.*

This is an example of fusion between health care and electronics, two unrelated fields that are now coming increasingly closer. The point to note here is that innovation by fusion happens through the mixing of *different* domains to create a new by-product. Some examples are shown in Table 5.2.

These are some randomly selected domains, the purpose being only to explain the role of *fusion* in the conceptualization and creation of innovative products, using familiar objects. The matrix gives examples of the fusion of two domains spawning new concepts at their intersection.

Table 5.2 Innovation by fusion

	Health Care	**Entertainment**	**Sports**
Electronics	BP monitor	Video games	Hawk-eye (DRS)
	Ultrasound scanner	Home theater	Wearables
	Weight machine	PlayStation	eSports
Automobiles	Emergency Rescue Vehicle	Car Stereo	Formula racing
	ACLS Transport	Touch-screen MP3 player	Auto rallies
	Mobile clinics (rural)	Bluetooth speakers	Monster Truck

Exercise: *As an exercise, create a 10 × 10 matrix of fields that you are familiar with in everyday life like food, nature, music, architecture, science, transportation, adventure, furniture, health care, house, farming, education, sports, entertainment—quite literally anything—and at their intersection, jot the familiar product, or idea created by the fusion. Next step (more difficult)—any thoughts on what is possible but not yet introduced? You may come up with some completely new ideas. This is how many familiar products were sparked.*

In the context of business, fusion means mixing ideas and experiences from *different* functions and markets to create innovative products, services, processes, or models. Some functions may appear to be far too dissimilar to fuse, but there's always a scope for intersection. The geeks in R&D and the eagles in legal may seem to have nothing to contribute together. But think again. The robust patenting mechanisms that protect (and monetize) hard-earned intellectual property are devised by this union.

Fusion opens immense possibilities for the digital enterprise. Almost all the new-age trends around us are results of the *fusion* of digital technologies. And many more opportunities are waiting to be created. Fusion of digital technologies like social media, Cloud, BDA, mobility, and Internet of Things (IoT) leads to some striking possibilities.

Table 5.3 Fusion in the digital world

	Cloud	Big Data	Mobility	Social Media	IoT	Apps
Cloud	IaaS. PaaS. Shar-ed Com-puting	CEM	Mobile Banking	Shared Storage [Social Cloud]	Video Sur-veillance	Inter-active Gaming
Big Data	Facial Recog-nition	Storage. Correla-tion. Analysis	GPS Navigation (Google Maps)	Sentiment Analytics	Machine Learning	Decision Support Systems
Mobility	e-com-merce	Mobile BI	Freedom from devices and n/ws	Instant multimedia messaging	Connected Cars	Mobile Ent Apps (Sales-force,...)
Social Media	Chat-bots (Alexa)	Person-alized Cam-paigns	BYOD	Audio, Text, and Video Inst Msgng	Remote Health Monitoring	Lync Skype
IoT	Smart Homes	Disaster Warning (EWS)	IR Motion Trackers	IPv6 based social n/w of "things"	Machine-to-Machine Commn	Embed-ded Apps
Apps	SaaS	Data mining and BI Apps	Loca-tion-based Services	Facebook, Twitter	Custom IoT Apps	Sw pro-grams for mobile devices

The examples given in Table 5.3 are quite general, but if smart people from Business and Technology work together on this, there is no limit to the number of unique possibilities at *each* intersection. You can add other domains as well—devices, artificial intelligence (AI), blockchain, cyber security, and so on—to get even more exciting ideas.

Association

This technique builds on the fusion principle. The potential for generating more numerous ideas through fusion, cross-fertilization, and intersections is derived from a simple property of the human brain viz., it works through *association*. This is a detailed science, but it can be exemplified easily through this simple test:

Test: Enumerate 20 different uses of a string (or rope).

What did you come up with? More importantly, *how* did you go about it? If you leveraged the power of *association*, you would have done this in a jiffy. In this simple test, a rope could be *associated* with random themes like games (e.g., skipping, tug-of-war, finish-line), home (e.g., clothesline, drawstring), adventure (e.g., rock-climbing, fishing), jobs (e.g., packaging, firefighting, cow herding), and many more. Under each association, a myriad of rope-use possibilities exists, some quite innovative. This is far more rewarding than trying to make a *random* list of the uses of rope, as you can readily attest. The power of association makes innovation simple by foraging into the remote regions of your brain. Perfect it through practice and see the difference!

Association can bring out some great ideas in the enterprise environment too and raise the company to new heights of accomplishment. A well-guided and moderated association process with the right mix of participants can truly become the cradle of innovation for the company.

Table 5.4 shows a few examples of situations that could lend themselves to solution by successive associations.

The technique of association does not always impose the use of complex or multipart association keys. Simple words, symbols, animals/birds, gestures, and pictures can be used just as effectively. A familiar allegory uses the eagle as an association key to uncover some great leadership

Table 5.4 Multipart Association Examples

S. No.	Question	Example of Association Keys
1	How can you differentiate your offering in the market?	CLC Stages
2	How can you improve the end-to-end experience for HNI customers?	Moments of truth
3	How can you reduce customer churn in rural markets?	Demographic factors
4	How can the alignment between Business and IT be improved in the company?	Alignment Dimensions
5	What are the benefits of introducing product X in market Y?	Market segments
6	How should our business strategy be different this year?	Technology trends
7	What can we do to achieve more enlightened security behavior by employees?	Seven habits (Covey)[1]

qualities.[8] The idea is to generate numerous ideas by association with a familiar object, word, or form. There is no limit to the possibilities that association opens for stimulating the thought process.

Cross-Pollination

A slight variation on the fusion technique, cross-pollination can be used to generate numerous options using the one-to-many principle. Here, you pick a theme, say *Drivers of Market Growth,* and use it to *pollinate* a set of completely unrelated domains for spawning new ideas. In poetic imagery, the *theme* is the *bee,* and the *domains* are *flowers,* which are pollinated for extracting the *nectar* in the form of ideas. In Figure 5.9, the cross-pollinating *bee* (drivers of market growth) hops across a few *random flowers* (sports, music, etc.) to extract the *nectar* of ideas from each, leading to a broader cumulative set. *Sports* makes us think of competitiveness and teamwork, *military* of strategy and structure, and so on. You can use this recursively (e.g., *competitiveness* can be the next bee). Cross-pollination is based on the premise that through diversity comes variety.

There are numerous other techniques and tools available for triggering innovation to generate new ideas. A discussion on every one of these, while instructive, would take us far beyond the intended theme of this book. Some of the other common techniques that can be useful in generating innovative ideas and solutions are mentioned below. You may like to study some of these in greater detail from other sources.

Cross-boundary group work: Helps *cross*-functional teams constructively identify solutions to business and organizational problems, by breaking down barriers and fostering openness among participants.

Fishbone: Form of structured brainstorming, performed diagrammatically, to look for root causes.

Force-field analysis: Force field analysis is a way to encourage creative thinking by identifying forces that *help* and those that *hinder* the process of getting to the targeted outcome.

Lateral thinking: Lateral thinking is a creative approach to solving problems and generating ideas using not-so-obvious methods, rules, or steps, that is, by thinking out of the box. It is one of the most effective

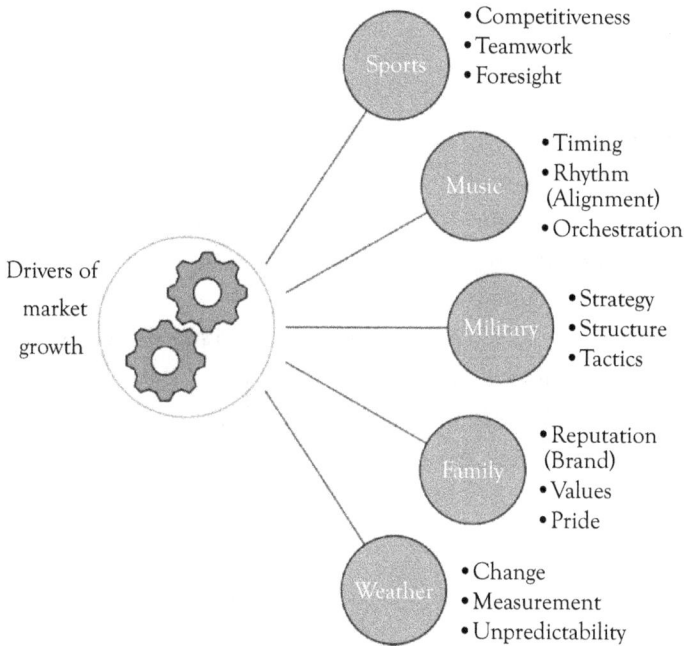

Figure 5.9 *Innovation through cross-pollination of ideas*

tools of creativity. For a detailed treatment of this, I recommend that you read Edward De Bono's book of the same name.[7]

List reduction: This is a way to logically process the output of a brainstorming session and reduce the number of options to a manageable quantity for further action.

Mind mapping: This is an individual technique. It enables one to generate and organize solutions around a central topic by capturing ideas along various branches and their off-shoots, like hubs and spokes.[9]

Outcome thinking: This is a creative process in which different participants visualize the *ideal* outcome of a situation and share their envisioned outcomes with other group members to reach a concise vision.

Pareto analysis: Pareto analysis is a great way to separate the "vital few" from the "trivial many." The familiar 80–20 rule is an example of this. It helps the group set priorities by ranking and presenting the data in a bar graph showing the distribution in descending order.

Storyboarding: Storyboarding is a visible process of gathering, evaluating, and organizing information. Participants jot down ideas on cards, which are put up on a visible board to select the most useful ideas, which are then progressively refined and built upon to reach the most workable set of solutions.

Structure tree: Structure tree is a systematic way of breaking down the theme into smaller, more manageable topics. They are useful in identifying and selecting problems to work on.

Swimlanes: As connected flowcharts of inputs, responsibilities, decision points, and output for a given plan or process, swimlanes can be an excellent way to find alternate paths to reach the stated outcome.

Irrespective of the technique or tool you adopt, always remember De Bono's first law: There is no such thing as the *best* idea. That is, innovation doesn't have a peak, so avenues for scaling higher are always open. Tools only help you find them faster.

Backbone and Empowerment

People whose emphasis is not on *succeeding* but on *not-failing* never make good innovators. Quite clearly, they are missing the *backbone*, that crucial prerequisite for innovation, without which great ideas cannot stand on their own. Haven't you ever come across the feeling, when an idea is applauded, that *you* could have done that but weren't sure it would be such a great one? If you want to ride the innovation wave, develop a backbone first: Do not be afraid to voice your ideas.

Related to this, organizations that have successfully leveraged the power of innovation are the ones that have given the *empowerment* to their teams to break free from the clutches and constraints, which prevent the free flow of ideas. The *dare-to-try* spirit *must* permeate the organization that is seeking to make a mark in the world as a digital enterprise. Backbone and empowerment cannot be substituted by any known tools or techniques as levers of human potential.

Applying Innovation

As we have discussed above, there are numerous tools and techniques available for stimulating creative thought. As you head into a territory where being different determines your chances of success and speed determines your survival, the importance of tools, techniques, and behaviors that expand *and* catalyze the thinking process indeed cannot be stressed enough. However, the specific tool or process that you employ is a matter of your comfort and the demand of your situation. You'll often find that it is a *combination*, rather than a specific technique, which works best.

Let us apply our simple tools and techniques of innovation to prepare your enterprise for its most important goal: *digital transformation*.

Digital Transformation

Digital transformation could take many forms and routes and could mean entirely different things, depending on the mode, mission, and means of the enterprise. However, there is one enduring feature that every digital transformation has at its core: A relentless drive for *innovation*. Therefore, the tools of innovation assume the role of tools of *transformation*.

Your ability as an enterprise to envision its digital future (i.e., have a compelling digital vision) is the real propulsion behind digital transformation. When planning for digital transformation, enterprises first decide upon the *key strategic objectives* (KSOs) under each of which the potential for value creation may be unlocked using innovation as the key, as shown in Figure 5.10. These KSOs essentially point the company in the direction it must take to digitally transform itself. Deciding the KSOs is best done by asking the question: *What must you transform (e.g., business model, customer experience, technology) to realize your digital vision?*

While the question seems simple enough, answering it may not be a trivial matter, as a mistake here would be an immeasurably costly one. A company aspiring to become a digital enterprise must weigh this question profoundly and comprehensively. Example 5.3 is about a striving company that was somewhat cavalier in the initial direction setting, eventually succeeding only in arriving at the wrong destination faster. There are both good and bad lessons to be learned from this example. You may like to use it as a case study with suitable alterations to suit your business circumstance. The case refers to a *hosted data center* focused on few large corporates, planning to transform into a full-fledged *public cloud service* (IaaS, PaaS, and SaaS) provider serving a much wider customer base, including SMEs and startups.

Example 5.3

A hosted data center provider traditionally provides passive IT resources like servers and storage along with associated power, cooling, and real estate to companies on a tenancy basis. Typical services to corporates include off-premise provision of IT infrastructure elements with SLA-based availability assurance, scale-up/down in real-time-based on business exigencies, colocation services, data security, and disaster recovery. These are billed as operational expense (opex) to the customers, providing freedom from capital investments, maintenance worries, and unpredictability of IT costs. The service is popularly known as Infrastructure-as-a-Service (IaaS). From the IaaS provider's perspective, it is a highly capital expense (capex) intensive business entailing considerable investments in real estate, power/back-up equipment, heating, ventilation and air-conditioning (HVAC), and IT infrastructure to serve multiple corporates, all expecting near 100 percent availability and round-the-clock efficient performance. The IaaS provider also incurs operational costs like equipment maintenance, electricity, fuel (for DG backup plants), and employee expenses covering salaries and overheads for business, technical, and other functions. Most IaaS providers maintain state-of-the-art and secure facilities with the latest systems and apparatus, which entail high costs.

Our company—we will call it XIP (Anonymous Infrastructure Provider) —hosted all the above data center services, having made substantial investments in its swank facility, infrastructure, and staff. The first two years were a period of growth for the company. Over time, XIP started facing challenges, which ranged from underutilized assets due to customers opting for public cloud, to increased competition, and higher overheads. The growth curve started dwindling. The company's promoters were rather unsympathetic, and the management decided to take strong steps to change course before it was too late.

The company called in a top consulting firm for advice. The consulting firm ("XCF") spent a couple of days looking at the company's strategy and performance and promptly suggested that XIP consider a renewed business model. This, they said, required diverse and innovative ideas and hence proposed an offsite brainstorming session. "Changing the business model" is increasingly considered a panacea for many of an organization's business troubles. However, it is easier said than done. How, precisely, do you go about this? Well, our XCF consultant had some ideas. Having got the XIP businesspeople into a room, he asked: "What are the top five things that must be done to improve the company's top line by 15 percent in 12 months?" A vigorous brainstorming followed, punctuated by a SWOT analysis, and by the end of the day, the group succeeded in building consensus on five of the many ideas that were generated, accepting that it would be "mission accomplished" if the team could act and deliver on these.

Six months into the project, it did not need a detailed formal review to conclude that the company was not going to deliver on its revamped strategy, nor achieve the much-touted turnaround. If anything, things were going more sharply southward than before. The signals were clear enough for the XIP management to go back to the consultant and rethink the business model. This time, though, they decided to use their internal think-tank, constituted of key Business and Technology folks, while the consultant was engaged only to facilitate and guide. The team reviewed the earlier ideas and concluded that though they were right from a technical revamp perspective, as they focused on virtualization, standardization, MPLS connectivity, security-firewall, and cost rationalization, they all simply built upon the existing edifice, not transform its scope. None of them, in hindsight, appeared a good enough reason to compel new customers to look at XIP.

After due deliberations, the root cause was traced to the initial question ("what are the top 5....?"), which itself postulated that XIP must somehow improve upon the current business only, instead of farming out in new areas. In other words, the focus was squarely on "What are we going to do?" rather than on "Who do we intend to be?" The XIP team brainstormed among themselves for the next half a day only to get to the right question that they must answer to recast their business. Finally, the question that was framed, with consensus, was: "What should be our value proposition for a differentiated customer experience in the on-demand information technology solutions segment?" There's no reference in the question to what, specifically, must be done, but on the identification of the focus areas, or the key strategic objectives. In the earlier question, the team had to rush into actionable solutions even before the problem had been identified!

The team then deliberated to generate a range of ideas in answer to this question. This was done using a combination of bucketization, fusion (cross-pollination), and brainstorming techniques to yield the maximum number of ideas.

The responses were then prioritized and grouped under the following three KSOs to guide the first phase of the company's transformation to a renewed business model:

- *Customer Experience*
- *Internal/External collaboration*
- *Value Proposition*

Having reached this far, the team was fired up sufficiently to drill down further and come up with innovative ideas for each KSO to create version 2.0 of the company. This entailed a collaborative model with ISVs to provide cloud-based application services, and thus expand its customer base to SMEs and entrepreneurs who found it cost-prohibitive to build/ buy their business applications like CRM and ERP. The company has so far shown positive results in its market performance, and I heard recently that its position has moved up a few notches in its industry space.

The above example shows that unless you first address the question of *which* areas need to be transformed to fulfill your vision, the transformation is an exercise in futility.

To reiterate, deciding on the KSOs is the critical starting point of your digital transformation journey. Figure 5.10 depicts the high-level blueprint for digital transformation. While typical, this is not universal. The real transformers of *your* business must be carefully and consultatively decided, using the various innovation techniques at your disposal.

For each KSO, it may be required to have a dedicated session (or workshop) to produce as many opportunities as possible, using any of the innovation tools, like fusion or cross-pollination. The process may be done recursively. For example, the "business model" KSO throws up

BLUEPRINT FOR ENTERPRISE DIGITAL TRANSFORMATION

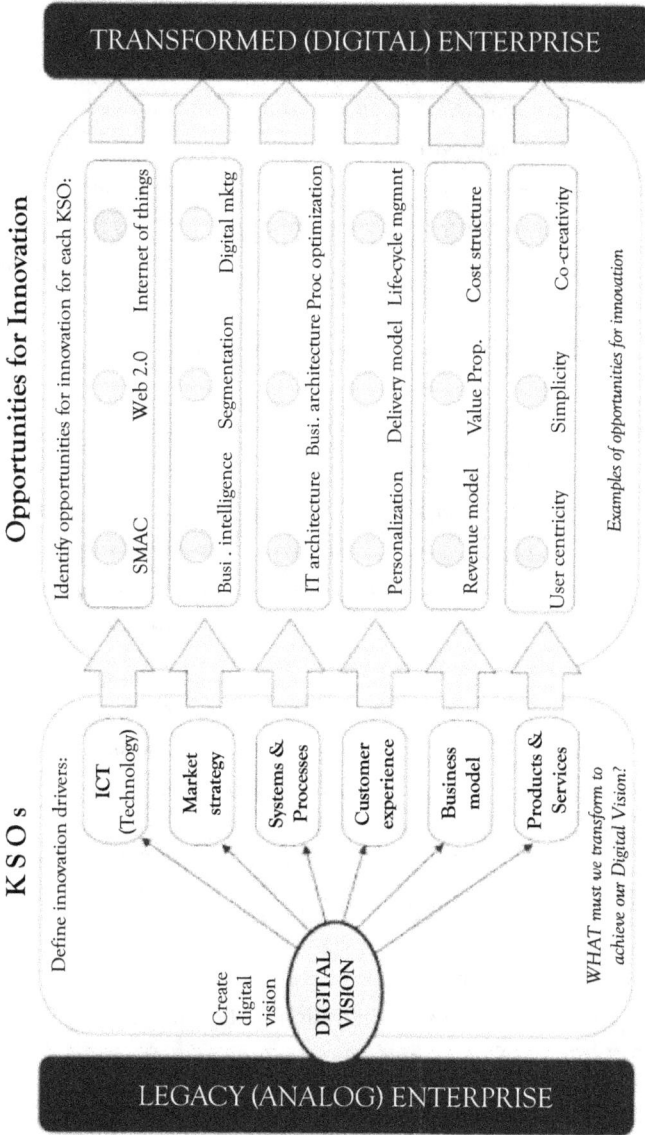

KSOs

Opportunities for Innovation

TRANSFORMED (DIGITAL) ENTERPRISE

Identify opportunities for innovation for each KSO:

Define innovation drivers:

ICT (Technology)	SMAC	Web 2.0	Internet of things
Market strategy	Busi. intelligence	Segmentation	Digital mktg
Systems & Processes	IT architecture	Busi. architecture	Proc optimization
Customer experience	Personalization	Delivery model	Life-cycle mgmnt
Business model	Revenue model	Value Prop.	Cost structure
Products & Services	User centricity	Simplicity	Co-creativity

Examples of opportunities for innovation

Create digital vision

DIGITAL VISION

WHAT must we transform to achieve our Digital Vision?

LEGACY (ANALOG) ENTERPRISE

Figure 5.10 Template for digital transformation

"value proposition," which may again yield to the cross-pollination technique (say) to generate more specific ideas, and so on.

Digital transformation, like any business transformation, is a very serious matter for an enterprise. Each KSO could be a long, arduous, and expensive journey requiring intricate planning, strategizing, and executing. Choose wisely.

The enterprise's *digital vision* is converted into individual KSOs (*transformers* or *innovation drivers*) through a collaborative effort involving Business and Technology stakeholders. In other words, all the transformers derive their power from a common source, which is the organization's *digital vision*. The opportunities for innovation identified here need not be all realized at the same time. Depending on the priorities of the enterprise, these may be applied in a phased manner.

Conduct a workshop to identify the transformers (KSOs) of your Business. (It will be among the most important exercises you will do as an organization.) *Spot the opportunities for innovation for each KSO. Prepare a display showing transformers and corresponding opportunities with real bulbs and switches against each opportunity, in your boardroom (your in-house electrician can do this). Get the individual transformation champions and innovators to switch-on a light bulb against an opportunity when the predefined threshold for it is crossed. Make it a ceremony! As a variation, you may use rotary dimmers instead of switches. This keeps innovation happening continuously, and the transparency of the results keeps motivation levels high as well.*

BITA for Innovation

Through this chapter, we have breezed through some techniques, tools, and applications that foster innovation in the enterprise, all of which rely on BITA being firmly entrenched in the enterprise core. We saw that many of the qualities that are critical for BITA are also needed to construct the platform for innovation. These include collaboration, empowerment, a shared vision, business and technical competence, customer centricity, and a two-in-a-box approach to markets. This brings us to an important deduction: Innovation is the synthesis of *all* the BITA dimensions—culture, strategy, structure, processes, tactics—working in tandem. Infusion of BITA into the organization's veins is, therefore, vital for innovation.

The typical question that does the rounds at some or the other point in most organizations is: Are we ready for the future? Almost without exception, the (honest) answer is No, because there is no perfect state of readiness to meet the demands of an unknown and uncertain future. The question to ask is: Have we achieved convergence of Business and Technology to take advantage of future opportunities and trends? It's principally about *alignment*.

In the context of the modern enterprise, there is no bigger platform for innovation than its digital transformation. The companies that accomplished their digital transformation journeys successfully did not rely on path-breaking greenfield innovations but on exploiting the existing trends—cloud, social, mobility, Big data—and supplementing them with layers of incremental, garden-variety innovation.

The scope and potential for innovation are both limitless. We started this chapter with predictions that could have halted humanity in its tracks but couldn't. Simply because they failed to dampen the human urge to explore, experiment, and embrace new paradigms, and achieve breakthroughs that succeeding generations have not only benefitted from but improved upon. It's a continuous cycle. There is no question that many path-breaking innovations—like drones and flying cars, autonomous vehicles, hyper-connectivity, cheap renewable energy, stem cell research, longevity, among others—are going to severely impact our lives and business in the not-so-distant future. Those who can blend and fuse these with other technologies to create innovative offerings are going to be the leaders of tomorrow. That's for sure. The real question is, how do *you* transform yourself to take advantage of the opportunities that innovation unearths? And the answer is: *Align* first. Innovation and transformation are simply a natural consequence of robust and sustained alignment.

CHAPTER 6

The Functional Focus

"If you want to go fast, go alone. If you want to go far, go together."

Alignment between Business and Technology to take advantage of the opportunities created by the digital economy has been our primary focus in this book. As an exponent of BITA for many years, I have found enthusiastic support for it both in word and spirit in most organizations, especially as the role of technology in business has intensified. However, I also came up with a fair share of skepticism based, as deeper probing revealed, on individual biases and preconceptions. Let us examine some of the common preconceived ideas (PIs) about BITA.

PI # 1: *An excessive focus on alignment could result in diluting the emphasis on functional priorities.* After all, Business and Technology are distinct functions with goals and deliverables of their own. By stressing BITA, one may wonder, are Business and Technology trespassing into each other's territory and moving away from their core functional charters? Therefore, is BITA somehow *weakening* the organizational pillars that were painstakingly built over the years, rendering the organization more vulnerable to external threats?

This is a point of view that comes from being entrenched too deep and too long in silos, breeding insecurities and threats, which can wreck BITA. The truth is that BITA is not a substitution device, but a force multiplier. In a BITA-centric organization, Business and Technology *reinforce* each other, achieving *more* than they could individually. Therefore, functional charters and core competencies are, in fact, strengthened by BITA.

PI # 2: *In the digital enterprise context, Business and Technology are indistinguishable, so alignment is a given.* Business and Technology indeed must be indistinguishable to the outside world in this Digital Age. However, this does not mean that they are functionally indistinct. While they do share a mission, Business and Technology have individual strategic outlooks, competence makeups, and even tactical stances. This is conducive to diversity of thought and action. *Distinct* but *aligned* Business and Technology functions are *required* to broaden the organization's horizons and enable it to take a more holistic approach to market and customer issues. An organization that takes a desegregated approach in its internal structure would thus be lacking the breadth required to take advantage of the opportunities in the market. In conclusion, this PI is unfounded and at the very best, unrealistic.

PI # 3: *Alignment is an old and overused fad, no longer relevant in this age of innovation.* I was quite surprised to hear this from no less than the CIO of a company. If anything, alignment is a *prerequisite* for innovation! So where could such a sentiment spring from? I have a few theories. First, catch phrases are annoying. Words like "alignment," which are often heard, are equated to jargon, and this tends to diminish their role and importance in our minds. However, overused does *not* mean irrelevant. Second, it is possible that the folks who view alignment as no longer relevant imagine that they have already attained nirvana and aspire nothing higher. Does such a state even exist? Even if we hypothesize that it does, the need to *retain* this coveted berth would render alignment anything but irrelevant. Third, companies where BITA is induced through coercion are the ones that see it as a fad. These are companies where alignment is force-fitted into the culture, while mutual suspicion and distrust rule.

PI # 4: *Technology is that faceless, behind-the-scenes, "maintenance-centric" entity, which has no scope for aligning with the customer-facing Business function.* It is sad but true that there are still people who view Technology through an extremely narrow lens, and in whose worldview, the above description could be just about right.

The other day, a young data analyst with a renowned airline told me how she almost slipped on sending out a critical report due to a glitch in her laptop. "So what did you do?" I asked her. "I just took the laptop to IT to have a look at it," she said. "And what is IT?" I asked. "Oh, it is that window near the reception on the 6th floor where you hand over your laptop so they could figure out the problem and fix it"! This is almost a verbatim conversation.

Let me emphasize again: IT is *not* just a maintenance window, but the sum of all activities that leverage technology for the fulfillment of the company's obligations to its stakeholders. Thus, in the above case, the lady who took her laptop to "IT" is herself as much a part of IT as the faceless person behind the window. Throughout this book, our definition of IT (or Technology) has included software and hardware engineering professionals (e.g., architects, developers, integrators), technical consultants, subject-matter experts (e.g., security, compliance), analysts, project managers, *and* the user support professionals responsible for the upkeep of IT infrastructure.

The notion that Technology is "faceless," "narrow," or "maintenance-centric" is reflective of a mindset that is not equipped to tap into the opportunities that a more inclusive definition of Technology opens.

The reason for bringing up some of the misconceptions (PIs) about the Technology function and its alignment with Business is that they could have a serious negative impact on the company's ability to emerge as a successful digital enterprise, which rests on a bedrock of BITA. These misconceptions stem from a failure to accept the enlarged role of Technology in the creation of business value. *Functional transparency* and *alignment* have decisive implications in determining the fate of the new-age enterprise.

The function of Technology is to make the business successful. Therefore, one of the primary functions of leadership in the new economy must be to remove every barrier in the alignment of Technology with Business. This calls for a shift from the pure technologist stance that IT leaders tend to define themselves by. During an interview at a CIO forum, I touched on some aspects of the IT leadership role in the new economy.[13] Excerpts:

Example 6.1

Q: Your advice to aspiring CIOs?

My advice to aspiring CIOs would be to expand their horizons beyond technology. It is not easy as that's our comfort zone with most of our lives spent in it. But to cross the same hurdles as I have, it is important to relate to business in particular and people in general. Feel their pain and be a trustworthy partner in their mission. Technology is just a tool to sculpt your masterpiece, not the masterpiece itself.

Also, do not ever lose sight of your statement of purpose, which is simply this: IT exists to make the business succeed. This is unchangeable. You can define your own path but don't ever lose sight of this goal. Ensure that this is demonstrated in the day-to-day behavior of the entire IT workforce, which includes your partners. Finally, never expect a quiet moment! Enjoy the roller-coaster. But maintain a healthy work–life balance to ensure you have the required charge to keep surging ahead.

Q: The biggest lessons learned in professional career?

I have been fortunate to have experienced the full length of the technology value chain in my professional career with some very renowned Indian and global organizations, from R&D to sales. We tend to define and differentiate ourselves by our professional expertise in a technical domain. However, every technology becomes obsolete or irrelevant, and then so do we. So lesson one is, change is inevitable—embrace it. Many of us at this stage are leaders of people. When you are hiring, counseling, or appraising, your actions may have purely business- or work-related significance for you. But for the person on the other side of the table, it means their future, their family's aspirations, and sometimes their whole life. It is not good to be emotional, but empathy is certainly required. Not only to be felt but displayed. Hence lesson two is, compassion is human—show it. Lastly, be it in our profession or our life, it is important to have an unshakable aim. It is vital not to be driven by objectives ("what am I going to do?") but by an ultimate goal ("who do I intend to be?"). That's the third and most important lesson I have learned.

Q: Five traits of highly effective CIOs?

The CIO role is not just about technology, project execution, and cost management but also about people. A CIO must see himself or herself as a business leader, whose sole mission is to make the business successful. First, a highly effective CIO derives the goals and priorities for the IT organization directly from the business goals. He or she ensures that every person in the team is an empowered stakeholder in the business outcome. Second, he or she does not believe that only seniority and experience bestows wisdom and is keen to learn from everyone, particularly the younger generation. Third, he is passionate about his work. The CIO's role is less about what he does and more about what he inspires. Being passionate about one's goals is the best form of inspiration one can provide. Fourth, he picks and leads an energized team, driven by extraordinary commitment. It always works from the top down. And fifth, he takes a great deal of pride in his work. He knows he plays a very constructive role in shaping the future of the business as well as the larger community. He also knows that there was never a better time to be a CIO, given the influence of information technology in people's lives.

Q: Tips for work–life balance?

Frequent recharge is very crucial, but to avail it, you need to ensure undisturbed breaks. Hence a strong second line is essential. Equally, an ability to prioritize well and focus on the important, resisting the urge to be pulled into crisis management, will ensure that, on a routine basis, you avail quality time with family and friends. Use your time during the day well so you can leave the office at a reasonable hour. Recognize your capacity and remind yourself that your effectiveness is a direct function of your health, especially as you grow in years. Plan your vacations in advance with your family and intimate your office well ahead. It is preferable to take two or three shorter breaks in the year than a single long one.

Q: Success parameters for CIOs/IT leaders in any organization?

Being a direct stakeholder in the creation of business value is the surest success parameter for IT leaders. Other critical success factors would include your peer relationships, networking within your industry, and your grasp on technology, which enables you to steer the organization through the surrounding technical maze. The ability to deliver on committed time, cost, and quality targets is a very important success measure for IT leaders, as is the demonstrated capacity to recover quickly from catastrophic situations, which are unfortunately a part of an IT leader's backdrop.

Leadership is the capacity that translates an organization's vision into reality. With the advent of the new economy, this idea has not changed. However, the style of leadership has undergone a vast transformation. Most notably, leadership is not about command and control, but inclusiveness (Figure 6.1). The leader's job is primarily to ensure that all barriers are removed to pave the way for the vision to be realized. This means that the Business and Technology leaders must focus on creating an enabling environment for their functional priorities to be in sync. It is important

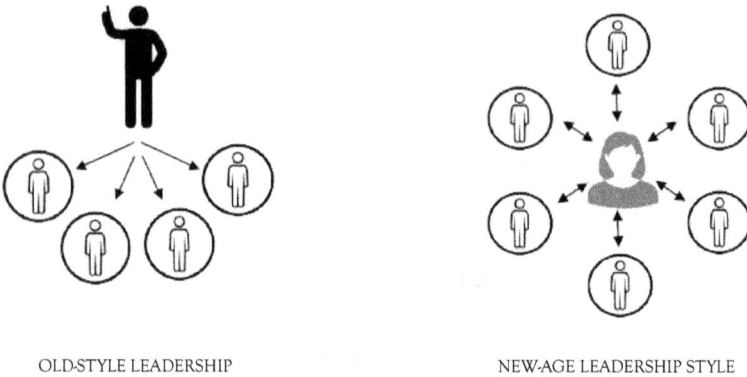

OLD-STYLE LEADERSHIP   NEW-AGE LEADERSHIP STYLE

Figure 6.1 Old and new leadership style

to reiterate that Business priorities are *market-driven*, so it is the responsibility of *Technology leadership* to assure continuous functional alignment between Business and Technology.

Functional alignment between Business and Technology happens when Business can profitably consume what Technology produces. Every work product of Technology, therefore, must pass the test of contributing to business gainfully. Every decision, policy, and action of Technology must be able to answer with an emphatic "yes" to the question: Does this add present or future *value* to the business?

In a nutshell, functional alignment is about defining and maximizing the *Business value of Technology*. To bring this into perspective, Business and Technology must have convergence on their response to the following questions:

1. What *benefit* must Technology produce to be of value to the business?
2. At what *cost* must Technology produce this value to the business?

The benefits and costs are not just in economic terms, but are a composite of many factors, determined together by the Business and Technology teams, and expressed as an index, or number. In its simplest expression, the Business value of Technology (or IT), which we shall call **BVIT**, is the combined *benefits* minus the overall *costs*. This, of course, implies that in a BITA-driven Technology organization, everyone—from the top leadership down—must make it their mission, above all else, to achieve two uncomplicated goals:

- Maximize the benefits of Technology to Business
- Minimize the cost of Technology to Business

Obviously then, determination of Business value of Technology concerns itself with finding ways to *measure* the benefits of Technology to Business, and the cost of Technology to Business. BVIT could be expressed as simply B–C (where B is the composite benefits, and C is the composite cost), or as B/C, or some other agreed expression. It is entirely up to the participants to define the formula through some nifty out-of-the-box thinking. What is important is an agreement between Business and Technology, and consistency in the measurement process so that trends can be observed.

BVIT brings out the impact of Technology on the performance and growth of *Business*. Internally focused measurements by IT can, at their best, have nil or very negligible positive impact on Business and at their worst, mislead Business due to misinterpretation or false-positive indications. They point to a clear divergence in functional priorities or impenetrable silos, which prevent any form of functional interlock. In either case, this goes against the grain of BITA.

Example 6.2

This example refers to a company whose major strength was technology, which it utilized to achieve excellence in customer delivery and managed services. The company decided that these technology capabilities, which influenced a significant part of the customer lifecycle, must be promoted as a differentiator for business leverage.

The teams, led by the Chief Technology Officer (CTO), got down to work on highlighting the company's delivery and technology accomplishments and soon had an impressive compilation. The aspects that went into the final presentation included details about:

- *Initiatives taken toward virtualization and the resulting benefits like efficient capex utilization*
- *Measures used to optimize development effort in R&D through techniques like theory of constraints, reuse*

- *Remote infrastructure management (RIM) facility to boost efficiency and the resulting reduction in time and cost (effort) to close service requests*
- *Improvements achieved in various performance measures for service requests and call tickets*
- *Performance statistics of key applications and tools for supporting customer operations*
- *Architecture diagrams showcasing modularity and the use of standard components and interfaces*
- *Statistics on Continuous Measurable Improvement (CMI) and quality at various stages of the development lifecycle*

Quite obviously, the narrative is not customer centric. First, an undue emphasis on complex technical terminology is a turn-off, as flaunting confusing terms to impress the customer only serves to alienate. This often happens with ads by technology companies. Second, the emphasis above is on showcasing the competence and perspective of the Technology teams, rather than on real benefits to the customer! While the customer may indeed be interested in knowing that there is proper oversight of the technology functions that serve him, what he is paying for is the benefit that accrues to his organization. Obviously, the question "What's in it for the customer?" was either glossed over completely, or it was assumed that somehow the customer would figure this out from the information provided. This is a very common mistake. If you were a customer, would your decision be materially swayed by the above presentation?

Functional alignment is not about doing what is right for Technology, but about breaking the shell to focus on what *matters to the Business*. In the above example, while all the bulleted actions are "right," they fall short of being directly relevant to the Business. It would be very hard for a Business team member to tie back most of these aspects to real business benefits. And even harder for the customer.

Exercise: Can you list five things that the above company should have focused on reporting, which would have genuinely improved the customer's perception and helped the business succeed?

Functional alignment refers to Business and Technology being equal stakeholders in the achievement of business outcomes. Unlike in the previous example, the functional priorities of IT must be derived from the *business* focus rather than the internal measures to improve productivity or efficiency. The focus, therefore, must be on business outcomes such as user acceptance results during pilot run, order-fulfillment cycle time, stage-wise customer experience parameters, and ability to customize solutions to individual customer needs, among others.

Therefore, functional alignment is about Technology understanding the functional priorities of the Business and modulating its goals and priorities to remain in continuous sync with them. This implies that functional alignment is *unidirectional*. That is, functional priorities of Business, which aligns with *market priorities*, determine functional priorities of Technology and *not* the other way (Figure 6.2).

In the early stages of IT, computer systems were routinely rendered inoperational for reasons outside the customer's control, such as technical malfunctions lasting days, spare parts nonavailability, delayed bug fixes, and imperfect recovery systems. Everything was offered on a "best-effort" basis. Looking back, it is easy to recognize that Technology's functional constraints had the power to decide, and often derail, business plans. This was probably among the chief reasons that Technology did not emerge as a real enabler of the business in its earlier avatars. No one trusted Technology to be a value creator for the business, as it was perceived to be an agency fixated on its internal priorities.

Cutting to the present, such a scenario is inconceivable. The functional objectives of Technology are now determined by the level of experience that you aspire to deliver to your *customer*. With some IT services,

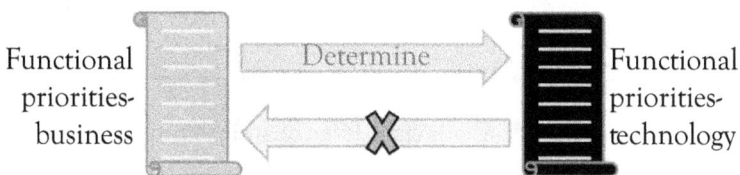

Figure 6.2 Unidirectional functional alignment

like SaaS, being run on the lines of utility services (like water and electricity) the functional goals of Technology can no longer be derived without keeping the functional goals of the Business in mind.

Exercise: List at least five functional priorities of the IT, Technology, or service unit of your organization that can be directly traced to the functional priorities of your business unit or customer.

We will now turn our attention to the determination of BVIT, one of the cornerstones of functional alignment. This has been defined by pundits, including Gartner,[10] in many ways, which are no doubt quite well-researched and worth emulating. Feel free to use the method that best suits your context. My simple premise is that to determine *value*, one must have a clear notion of two factors: *benefits* and *cost*. Without one, the other is meaningless, as this simple example demonstrates.

Example 6.3

I remember this incident from a sales training program I attended many years ago. At one point, the facilitator took out a black box neatly tied in ribbon and kept it on the table where everyone could see it. Then he said, "I am willing to give this away for $100. Any takers?" He didn't say what was in the box. No hands went up. Obviously, people wanted to know what they were getting for their money. He then said, "OK—here's my last offer. I will give this away for $50. Any takers now?" Still, no one came forward. After some atmospherics, he opened the box, and to everyone's surprise, there was an elegant and expensive wristwatch inside, costing not less than $250! He again asked, "Any takers now?" All hands went up! What had changed? It was the same box and content, the same price, and the same aspirants. The only difference was that now both the cost as well as the benefit were visible and hence people could appreciate the value of the deal. The point here is that it is never the cost alone, or the benefit by itself, that determines value, but their combination.

BVIT also works on this principle. It is a quantifiable measure derived from an assessment of the benefits *and* cost of Technology to the Business. Of course, no reduction technique exists that can precisely convert an experience into a number, so a certain amount of subjectivity is inbuilt in the measurement. However, if the measurement is done using the same principles over extended periods, it's an excellent compass in the journey to functional alignment.

The Benefits Basket

The first step toward determining BVIT is quantifying the *benefits* of Technology (the term Technology, as in the rest of this book, includes all the functions involved in technology development, delivery, and operations). The benefits of Technology to Business may be measured and reported in the following buckets to arrive at the composite *Technology Benefits Index*.

- **Customer engagement** (*Enhancing credibility* by fulfilling the obligations to customers/ markets)
- **Service excellence** (*Creating distinction* through superior delivery and operations of technology services)
- **Economic contribution** (*Improving profitability* through influence on financial performance)
- **Technology readiness** (*Building capability* to take advantage of the digital opportunity)

Almost all the benefits of Technology that are relevant to BVIT typically fall under one of the above heads in my experience, though some obliquely. The important point here is to find a *consistent* methodology for quantifying these benefits.

Customer Engagement

The extent to which Technology identifies with and embraces issues that directly impact the *end-user* or *business* is a measure of its customer engagement. For example, the report from IT that shows a month-on-month reduction in insurance claim processing time, or the increase in customer churn along with root causes, or the end-to-end order-to-delivery time, is an indicator of its customer engagement. Depending on your industry segment and business direction, the set of customer engagement metrics could be quite diverse.

Customer engagement is not just about reporting of relevant information. Tools and systems must be prebuilt to *capture* the required data at the right time, assimilate it, and present it in a comprehensible format to the Business. Based on the information presented, Technology (or IT) must be able to institute actions to tune the outcomes to business aspirations. Tools that extract information on-the-fly from business applications are referred to as *hooks*. These hooks are developed by IT for obtaining business-critical information at all stages.

Let us take the example of a mobile telecom operating company, and some features that all of us, as users (customers) of mobile services, are familiar with.

As can be noted from Table 6.1, which is an example of IT's customer engagement, unless there are hooks built into the IT systems to extract relevant data, such metrics cannot become a reality (e.g., #4). This requires that Business–Technology alignment is factored-in during the *design* and *development* of IT systems. If this is not embedded, you may have to build this using a change request to write internal or external code. Most often, the target values are *parameterized* and can be changed. In the case of metric #1, for example, the horizon may be changed from 30 to 25 seconds.

Table 6.1 Monthly IT Report (illustrative sample)

SN	Metric	Unit	Target	Achvmt^	Score
1	Average call waiting time at service desk	seconds	30	87.0%	87
2	Prepaid recharges (end-to-end) completion time	seconds	60	99.0%	99
3	Customer activation time	hours	4	65.0%	65
4	Voice calls completed without getting dropped	%	99.9%	99.8%	99
5	Average C-SAT rating for Service Requests handling	Out of 5	4	4.3	108
6	Postpaid bill accuracy (Error bills/1000)	Number	1.0	0.9	111

[^Achvmt: Achievement. For #1-3, % of cases completed within target. For #4, actual percentage. For #5 and #6, value averaged over all cases.]

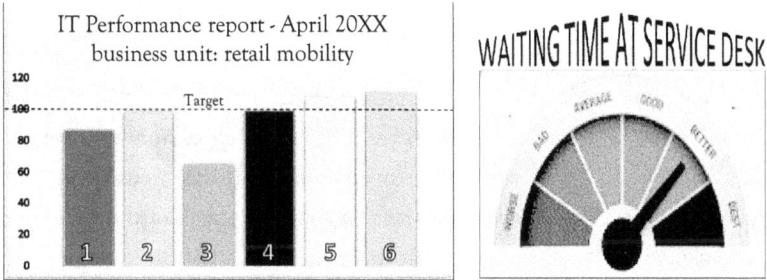

Figure 6.3 IT Customer engagement index

Such flexibility ensures that Business and Technology stay functionally aligned even as customer and market expectations fluctuate.

The scores on the customer engagement parameters are plotted in the bar graph in Figure 6.3. It is reflective of IT's grasp on issues impacting the customer, and its ability to measure and report these. While the focus is on maximizing the overall value (i.e., the weighted average, which is 0.95 in this example), attention to *individual* metrics cannot be overlooked. For example, you may pull up the average by further improving the postpaid bill accuracy (#6). However, it will do nothing to assuage the feelings of folks who must wait more than 30 seconds for their voice to be heard (#1), or the new subscribers whose connections get activated (#3) after their patience wears out! A monthly trend graph (like Figure 6.4) on each parameter lends invaluable insight into the direction of movement as an impetus to timely course corrections.

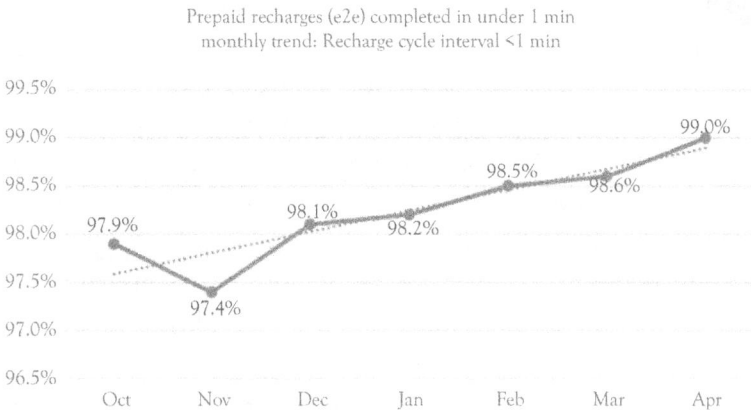

Figure 6.4 Trend report

The metrics in the above example pertain to *direct* actions by IT that have an impact on the company's competitive positioning. IT can also add to business value by facilitating the capture, retrieval, and analysis of data that *helps the Business to more effectively execute on its customer strategy.* In the above scenario, this could include churn analysis, customer segmentation, and experience parameters at different stages of the customer lifecycle. Virtually, there is no limit to the value that IT can create for the Business by leveraging its most important asset: Information.

Service Excellence

Service excellence is a benchmark that imparts confidence to the Business that the service machinery is well oiled and able to deliver on business commitments, both internal and external. It starts with close engagement between Business and IT to agree on the service and performance targets of the deliverables from IT for meeting the expectations of the market.

The two aspects of IT that significantly impact service excellence are its delivery and operations capabilities. Delivery has a direct bearing on the schedule, development cost, and quality (features, performance) of the final product or service. IT operations, on the other hand, have a significant impact on customer retention, requiring IT to not only render excellent service but also capture, process, and correlate experience parameters at every stage of the lifecycle. IT operations also ensure that internal IT systems required for secure and smooth business functioning are seamlessly and transparently available where needed and when needed. Like oxygen.

Together, IT delivery and operations are the lifeline of the company, more so in this Digital Age. An ability to *measure* performance as well as trends of key delivery and operations parameters is crucial for business value creation. The service excellence metric, often referred to as IT quality index or service quality index, is a derivative of key Technology delivery and operations parameters. A few years ago, I had participated in the development of a composite indicator of IT service quality, which received wide interest across segments and was included in The Innovation Workgroup's annual yearbook among the top IT innovations.[11] It was a proud and satisfying moment, as it recognized the importance of IT delivery and operations metrics in leading the business to success.

Incidentally, in some companies the role of IT partners is central to IT delivery and operations. The IT partners are an extension of the organization's core IT function, and their services are considered to be part of IT's performance. The partner's role in such cases may be vital to the computation of delivery and operations indices.

Staying with our mobile company, let us consider an example to illustrate how service quality may be measured and reported.

As the first step, the company's Business and Technology functions deliberated upon the *delivery efficiency index (DEI)* that would guide the delivery course from Business Requirements (BR) generation to production roll-out. This was a detailed measurement calling for close engagement of Business and IT in deciding the key parameters that needed to be quantified and reported to enable the Business to make sensible predictions and rational, data-driven decisions. Table 6.2 lists the delivery parameters that Business and Technology agreed to track monthly for the DEI metric.

This is just an indicative chart. If some of the terms do not resonate with you, don't worry. The intent is only to clarify the concept of DEI at a broad level. The composite DEI may be taken as the weighted (if you assign different weights to individual metrics) or a simple average of the actual values, which works out to 88 percent, or 0.88 here.

It is useful to track the delivery parameters along the time, cost, and quality dimensions on a month-on-month basis. This requires an investment to build or buy requisite tools for accurate and unambiguous measurement. It is a worthy investment, with quick return on investment (RoI) through future savings in cost, quality, and goodwill. From Figure 6.5, which plots the values from the previous table, it is straightforward to see the attributes that are "under the weather" and need to be pulled up, at least for the month under advisement.

Aside from IT delivery, service excellence focuses on IT *operations*. Therefore, the company also identified key *operational* parameters that were simultaneously reported as *operations health index (OHI)* in the determination of the comprehensive service excellence index. Generally, the parameters that portray characteristics required to *change (or transform) the Business* are clubbed under delivery, and the ones required to *run the Business* are clubbed under operations. In both delivery and operations, there are facets that may be important but are *internal* to

Table 6.2 Delivery-efficiency index (DEI): Report for the month April 20XX. [Sample]

SN	Attribute	Metric	Target	Actual
B1	BRs	New Business Requests (BRs) raised during the month (added)		68
B2		BRs scheduled for delivery in the month (cumulative)		93
T1	Time	New BRs: Impact analysis (IA*) completion on schedule	98%	100%
T2		New BRs: On-time Business approval on cost and time estimates	95%	84%
T3		New BRs: Milestone compliance (T1*T2)	93%	84%
T4		Scheduled BRs: Release compliance (to prelaunch *user testing*)	95%	93%
T5		Scheduled BRs: User testing to *production* launch compliance	98%	98.5%
T6		Scheduled BRs: Overall schedule compliance (T4*T5)	93%	91.6%
C1	Cost	Effort adherence (against baseline plan) for scheduled BRs	90%	94%
C2		Effort saving due to reuse for scheduled BRs	20%	61% (of target)
C3		Cumulative (year-to-date) effort adherence (against plan)	90%	92%
C4		Cumulative (year-to-date) effort saving due to reuse	25%	75% (of target)
C5		BRs in actual use by Business/customer postproduction	98%	80%
Q1	Quality	Preproduction (user acceptance testing [UAT]) quality (BRs with 0 severe defects in UAT)	90%	90%
Q2		Production quality (BRs with 0 severe or major defects in <1 m)	99%	100%

IA is performed to appraise the Business of the impact of the BR on time, cost, and functionality.

IT, and the service excellence metrics does not include these. As with DEI, the first step in the determination of the operations health index was to agree on its constituents and the process of their measurement. The company decided on five operational parameters and their target levels for computing OHI, as shown in Table 6.3, with all parameters

IT DELIVERY EFFICIENCY-April 20XX
Business unit: TSP-Emerging markets

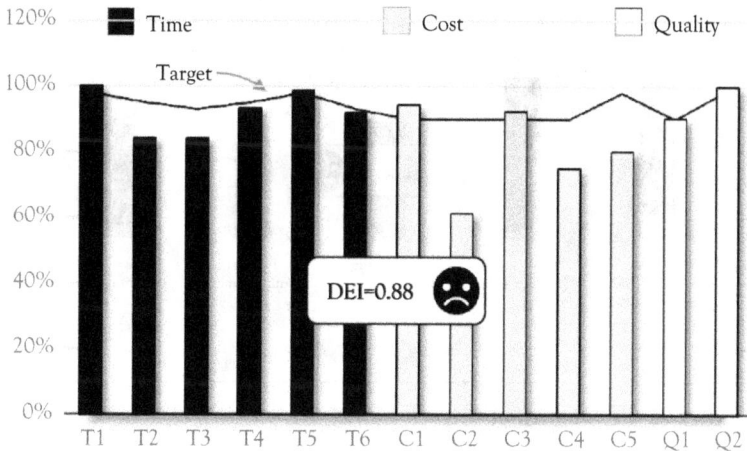

Figure 6.5 *IT delivery efficiency index*

having equal weight, though this can be varied. These results are plotted in Figure 6.6.

User Service Requests (USR) Resolution Index: This is an index to track the resolution of user tickets. A simple measurement could be <No. of User tickets resolved within SLA>/<No. of User tickets received>.

Applications Incidents Index: This measurement accounts for the availability of business-critical applications by tracking the uptime of these

Table 6.3 *Operations health index*

SN	Metric	Target	Curr. Actual	Prev. Actual
1	User Service Requests (USR) Resolution Index	0.98	0.99	0.98
2	Applications Incidents Index	0.95	0.96	0.96
3	Data Sanctity Index	0.85	0.71	0.70
4	Business Continuity Index	0.67	0.67	0.72
5	Information Security Index	0.90	0.86	0.82

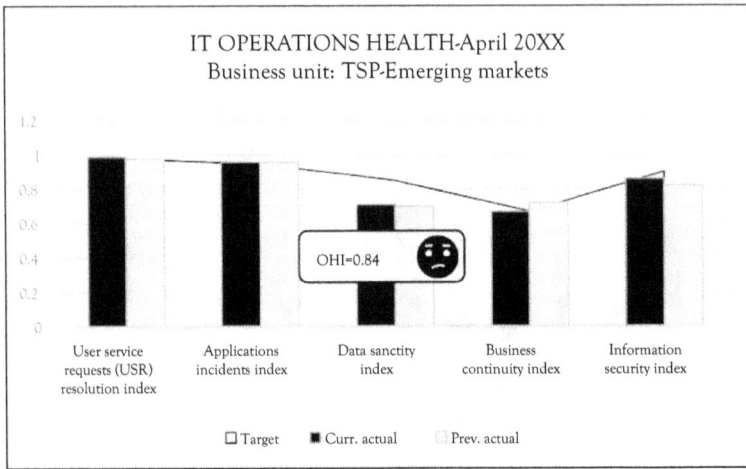

Figure 6.6 IT Operations health index

applications. For example, $< \sum(\text{uptime of Business apps [hrs]})>/<\text{No. of}$ Business apps*720>.

Data Sanctity Index: This is a tool-based measurement that checks for data synchronization across multiple databases as an indicator of the integrity of business-critical data, including customer data.

Business Continuity Index: This is a composite index derived from the measured performance levels, switch-over times, and overall performance of the *recovery* infrastructure (DR).

Information Security Index: Information security index is a measure of the efficacy of information security systems, computed by correlating security logs of reported and prevented incidents.

All values are normalized within a 0 to 1 range. Here we have taken OHI to be the *simple* average of the five parameters, that is, 0.84.

Every industry or enterprise may reach its own verdict on what must be measured (and how) for arriving at the composite OHI. Irrespective of what your list consists of, you will probably require special tools or hooks for accurate and objective reporting of the operational parameters.

Economic Contribution

Creation of business value is the primary *purpose* of Technology's existence and not merely a benefit. Everything Technology does (or *should* do) contributes to the business. The economic contribution of Technology to business is usually indirect, but there is also vast potential for *direct* economic contribution by Technology, which many new-age enterprises have successfully leveraged.

Example 6.4

Some years ago, I was heading the consulting and systems integration (CSI) division for a large European telecom gear maker in the fast-paced Indian telecom market. The division focused on customized offerings using integrated third-party products (which complemented the company's portfolio) to create complete solutions and had the dual responsibility of revenue generation and service delivery, operating as a regional Profit and Loss (P&L) unit. The entire CSI unit was identified as one of the divisions of the company's Service (or Technology delivery) organization. The CSI unit contributed directly to not just the company's bottom line, but also the creation of goodwill with highly discerning customers in an intensely competitive market. In this environment, characterized by largely similar companies with similar products, CSI was a refreshing break as it offered direct engagement between customers and Technology function to help build solutions that were specific to a customer. This led to improved collaboration with customers, often resulting in rewarding upsell opportunities. The trust and goodwill generated by CSI were also capitalized by other divisions of the company to boost sales. CSI, which was seen by some as a "gap filler," quickly metamorphosed into a "solutioneer." This is an example of the potential of Technology function to directly contribute to the business in enhancing economic value.

Despite examples like the above, the overwhelming view of Technology (IT) is still of a support function that can at best play a marginal and incidental role in creating economic value. It is difficult for most to conceive that Technology, in fact, *is* the Business. Like CSI, Technology can *directly* contribute to the growth of the business by becoming a source of incremental revenue and goodwill. The inhibitors are more often rooted in the cultural and attitudinal stances than in functional abilities or aptitude.

The other instance of economic contribution by Technology is where Business and Technology are two-in-a-box in their approach to economic value creation. Here, Technology is not an independent island but an equal stakeholder in the achievement of economic results, like revenue and profit after tax (PAT), carrying the same economic goals as the Business. It is not a best-effort scenario. Instead, Technology and Business are partners through *all* the stages of the *economic value creation process[12]* (Figure 6.7). They swim or sink together.

Instead of Technology coming in for support, like assisting with proposals or presentations, there is a *continuous* engagement of Technology at every stage of economic value creation, having shared goals toward the attainment of *business* results. This requires breaking the shackles and demolishing the silos to put *Technology in the front-end*, locking step with Business all the way to tap into the vast potential unleashed by the digital economy.

Economic value co-creation requires Business and Technology to focus together on the three simple, time-tested tenets of value creation:

1. **Sell what people *want* to buy**. Customers don't buy products or technology. They buy *experiences* delivered via products or technology.
2. ***Always* Deliver on your promise.** To be successful, you must only promise what you can deliver, and deliver more than you've promised.
3. **Do it *better* than your competition.** Competition is a good thing. It gets you out of complacency. Remember that somebody can as do it better, and that somebody is *you*.

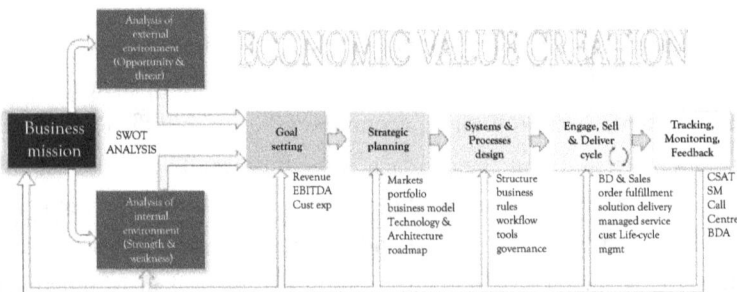

Figure 6.7 Economic value co-creation

The economic contribution index (ECI) is a measure of (1) direct economic value addition by Technology and (2) indirect economic value added by Technology through functional integration with Business. The direct economic value addition by Technology is the *actual* contribution of Technology to business, against a given business *target* (like sales quota, or profitability target) through direct selling, or upselling. It can be a simple measurement (say, actual-revenue/target-revenue) or, preferably, a combination of several weighted factors such as revenue, profitability, and C-SAT to arrive at a composite value, as shown in Table 6.4.

This sample gives a weighted average score of $(40\% \times 0.80) + (40\% \times 1.17) + (20\% \times 0.95) = 0.98$

Again, this is only one of the many possible ways to specify direct business contribution by Technology.

Table 6.4 Direct economic contribution

	Factor	Weight	Target	Actual	Achievement
a	Revenue	40%	USD 1m	USD 800K	0.80
b	Profitability	40%	15%	17.5%	1.17
c	C-SAT Score (scale of 5)	20%	4	3.8	0.95

Next, let us take the *indirect* contribution. As we touched upon earlier, this may require *stage-wise* measurement of Technology contribution based on the economic value creation model. Or, one could simply use the *three-point rule* that we just discussed. That is, quantifiably determine the indirect contribution by Technology as a response to the following questions:

1. What is the contribution of Technology in *creating* the experiences (products, services, technology) that customers are willing to pay for?
2. What is the contribution of Technology in *delivering* on the commitments made throughout the customer lifecycle?
3. What is the contribution of Technology in bringing the *differentiation* that keeps your organization ahead of the competition?

Assessing and quantifying the responses may require breaking each question into four or five constituent questions that are unique to an enterprise environment. A simple template is used to capture the feedback from Business on a scale of 1 to 5. For simplicity, let us consider all questions to carry the same weight here. If the average of all responses to questions under 1, 2, and 3 are 4.1, 3.9, and 3.6 respectively, the indirect contribution score would be 3.87 on a scale 5, which is 0.77. This may be a good window into Technology's indirect contribution but may not always reflect *actual* business results. Hence this is linked to the *business* results (most often *revenue* achievement) to arrive at the *composite* index of indirect contribution by Technology. If the company's revenue achievement is at 90 percent of the target, the indirect business contribution index would be 90% × 0.77, or 0.69.

From the above, we have a direct ECI of 0.98 and an indirect ECI of 0.69. If direct contribution has a weight of 75 percent and indirect contribution has a weight of 25 percent, the composite ECI works out to (75% × 0.98) + (25% × 0.69), or 0.91. You can formulate your own ECI to suit your environment. The above is just one of many possible methods.

Technology Readiness

Giving the organization a sharp technological edge is perhaps one of the most vital and visible contributions of Technology to the enterprise. The degree to which technology is being applied by an enterprise impacts not just its ability to create economic and customer value, but also to attract investment and employment. Yet, it eludes direct measurement. If there is a problem today with technology, it is perhaps that there is too much of it! So, when does an enterprise have the *right* technology focus, and more pertinently, how does it *measure* its technology readiness? With so much riding on technology, its assessment cannot be consigned entirely to subjectivity. Therefore, a practical and straightforward way to gauge the adoption and application of technology for business value creation is the need of the hour.

A practical method of measuring technology adoption is to prepare a basic *template* listing all aspirational technology elements under suitable heads, as in Table 6.5. Through periodic surveys, benchmarks, and brainstorming, the template can be continually augmented to keep it as current as possible. The extent of adoption in the enterprise against each

Table 6.5 Technology readiness estimation

Focus Area	Category	Technology Element	Weight (0–4)	Score (0–5)
External (Business and Customer value)	Digital	Cloud-based business applications	3	4
		Hosted Cloud services/offerings for customers	3	1
		Enterprise mobility (devices, apps)	3	4
		Social media for tuning into Voice-of-Customer	2	1
		Instant messaging—business/customer network	2	4
		Big data analytics (real-time analytics)	1	2
		Digital platform (modular Architecture)	1	4
		e-Commerce platform and gateway	3	4
		Web-based (digital) marketing tools	3	1
		Self-care portal for web-based customer service	2	4
		Immersive technologies	0	0
	Industry-specific Tech (Banking)	Java applications (JVMs)	4	3
		Digital banking platform	3	4
		Multifactor cybersecurity platform	3	3
		Integration of Social Media (SM) platform	2	1
		Biometrics for authentication	3	1
		Digital wallet	3	2
		Blockchain	2	1
	Business Support Systems	Customer experience management (CEM)	4	3
		Customer lifecycle management	3	2
		Billing and payment	4	4
		Business data warehouse (DWH), BI	3	3
		Data extraction and mining	3	3
		Data visualization and presentation	2	3
		Revenue assurance and fraud management	4	4
		Data confidentiality, integrity, and availability	4	4

Internal (Productivity and Efficiency)	Digital	Enterprise mobility—BYOD	2	3
		Internal mobile apps (or) mobile intranet portal	3	3
		Cloud-based access to business apps and data	3	3
		Big Data analytics	2	2
	Enterprise Productivity	Enterprise resource planning (e.g., SAP, Oracle)	4	4
		RDBMS (e.g., Oracle 11g)	4	4
		Application integration (EAI, web-services, SOA)	3	2
		Functional tech—SCM, HCM, FMS …	3	0
		Information lifecycle management	3	1
		Enterprise software platform (e.g., Java EE)	3	4
		Architecture standardization (e.g., TOGAF)	4	2
	Enterprise communication	High-definition (HD) video conferencing (or) telepresence	3	0
		High-speed data communication network	4	4
		Video conferencing over web channels	4	4
		Secure instant messaging (e.g., MS Lync)	4	4
		Enterprise-class e-mail solution (e.g., Exchange)	4	5
	Infrastructure	Data storage and management system	4	4
		Application servers on private/public cloud	3	3
		Server/storage virtualization	3	4
		Security firewall	4	4
		Business continuity (DR)	4	4
		Operations support platform (e.g., Openview)	3	1
Future Readiness		Machine learning	1	0
		Artificial intelligence	1	0
		3D printing	0	0
		IoT / M2M	1	0

Thought Leadership	Learning	Training and development initiatives	4	5
		Tech seminars for Business and non-IT	3	3
		Technology-vendor-led consultations	3	3
	Knowledge Management (KM)	Knowledge management tools	3	2
		Empowered technology council	3	3
	Innovation	Encouragement of dare-to-try spirit	3	2
		Investment in prototypes and proof-of-concept	3	1
		Sandbox and incubation labs	3	1

element is objectively weighted and scored using a *defined rule set* (suggested later in this section) to arrive at the final index. Table 6.5 gives a template along with sample ratings, but it is entirely flexible. You may like to invest time in creating a list that is more pertinent to your environment and keep enriching it with time for greater precision. A customizable and automated version of the Technology Readiness measurement tool can be downloaded from the website www.alignedtowin.com.

The range of technologies and options is so vast that no list can be comprehensive. *You must carefully select the tech domains that are important for your business and construct your own template.* The above categories, technologies, weights, and scores are intended to be only a guide to point you in the general direction of technology measurement at an enterprise level.

The weights are assigned in accordance with preestablished rules, as, for example, in Table 6.6, to reduce ambiguity.

Table 6.6 Technology weights

0	The technology or domain is not (or no longer) relevant to my *industry segment*
1	The technology is relevant to my *industry* segment but not immediately crucial to my *business*
2	The technology is essential for creating *differentiation* in the market [enhances my business prospects, e.g., social media for tuning into voice-of-customer]
3	The technology is critical for ensuring the attainment of *strategic goals* [e.g., Business support system, CEM system, cybersecurity platform for banks]
4	The technology is vital for running the business operations more efficiently and securely [e.g., enterprise e-mail, security firewall]

Despite this classification, you may frequently have to make judgment calls for assigning weights. Stay with them—they usually work. If in doubt, choose the *highest* weight category. For example, "cloud-based access to business apps and data" may be relevant from the perspective of 2 as well as 4. Choose *4* here.

The weights that have been assigned above in the example list pertain to an enterprise in the *banking industry segment*. Depending on the environment, the weights may be reassigned because what is strategic to one may be simply an efficiency booster for another, and vice versa.

Similarly, a classification may help in assigning *scores* to each technology element in a less ambiguous manner. Again, there is no strict formula that would be applicable in every situation–just like for *weights*. You may create your own truth-table for score assignment, an *example* of which is given in Table 6.7.

Using this classification, the scores have been populated in Table 6.5. Having come this far, the derivation of the Technology adoption index (or TAI) is just a simple arithmetic task. Compute the weighted average score ($\sum(w^*s)/\sum(w)$, which comes to 2.86 out of 5 in our sample), getting 2.86/5, or 0.57 as the composite TAI.

With a reasonably comprehensive template, this method generally yields a TAI of 0.70 or less even for enterprises that are well advanced in their tech journeys. A target of around 0.60 is considered quite ambitious here.

Table 6.7 Technology scores

0	Does not exist currently, nor on the roadmap for at least one year.
1	Does not exist currently, but on the roadmap and budget for deployment in next one year
2	Under development or implementation, but not yet tested or moved to production environment
3	Launched and deployed for business operations for < 6 months
4	In active operation for over 6 months, but not upgraded to latest version of the technology
5	In active operation for over 6 months, presently running the most recent version of the technology

Table 6.8 Composite benefits index

SN	Index	Weight (%)	Target	Actual
1	Customer engagement (CEI)	20%	0.95	0.95
2	Delivery efficiency (DEI)	15%	0.95	0.88
3	Operations health (OHI)	15%	0.95	0.84
4	Economic contribution (ECI)	25%	0.90	0.91
5	Technology adoption (TAI)	25%	0.60	0.57
	Composite Benefits Index		**0.85**	**0.82**

Let us summarize what we finally have on the *benefits indices* scorecard, from the above sample computations. The composite technology benefits index (Table 6.8) is the weighted average of the component indices.

One way to plot the composite benefits index and the individual indexes is presented in Figure 6.8. Remember, trends are important.

Figure 6.8 Composite IT benefits index

The Cost Factor

As important as it is to have a grip on the *benefits* of Technology to business, on their own they fall short of determining the *value* of Technology to Business. The *cost* at which these benefits were attained could curtail the overall value. Moreover, the cost is not only financial or monetary but the sum of all the elements that increase the overhead of doing business. A holistic approach to BVIT requires incorporating both the benefits and *cost* factor in the calculation.

The most common categories of overhead costs associated with Technology are as shown in Table 6.9. The focus of both Business and Technology is, of course, on minimizing *each* element of Technology (IT) cost to Business.

Table 6.9 IT costs

Category		Examples of Cost Elements
Capital (money)	Incurred on	Hardware, software, personnel, outsourcing
Effort	For achieving	Access, response, speed, flexibility
Risk	Accepted toward	Security, compliance, obsolescence, regulation
Complexity	In dealing with	Structure, policy, process, technology

---

Example 6.5

On the highway that connects my home to the city, there is a toll plaza. This toll is a huge financial, physical, and psychological barrier to the smooth passage of vehicles. Every time I need to drive up to town, which is often, I must cross this toll plaza. The place is a nightmare. The money to be paid per trip, while it adds up to a substantial amount monthly, is the least of the botherations. The delay——or the time cost——is a huge factor, particularly when one is on the way to the airport, railway station, or a doctor's appointment. There is no predictability. Crossing this toll may take anything from 5 to 30 minutes each way as the tail-back often stretches a kilometer! Then there is the chaos. With no proper queuing system, there's breakneck competition among unruly drivers of assorted vehicles—including huge trucks, buses, dumpers, cars, and taxis—to reach the tolling booth. It's the law of the jungle. Lastly, you must contend with rude polling staff who take your money as if they are doing you a favor, in their own time. The toll operator sees no incentive in improving things for the very people who keep his cash registers ringing since he knows they have no choice. The mess at the toll, however, teaches us a few important lessons about the elements of cost. Clearly, the cost is not just monetary but includes all the four cost categories outlined above.

Exercise: Think of your own IT function. List down the various "costs," or the toll, that Business must pay to IT for realizing the benefits of IT in your organization. Note that not all the imposed toll may be intentional. It is advisable to take this up as a serious and open-minded exercise.

As the next step, draw out a plan to bring down the IT "toll" to the minimum possible level. You will see the Business value of IT spiral steadily upwards just through this simple exercise.

Staying with the exercise, can you *measure* these costs, or quantify them in a meaningful way? Unfortunately, most of the nonmonetary costs of Technology are based on experiences or perceptions and thus do not lend themselves to numeric computation. Devising nifty formulas or mathematical models to quantify them may, therefore, be misleading and counterproductive.

The *monetary* cost though can be measured, usually against the budgeted amount. Functional alignment requires that the IT budget is not a common pool for everyone to dive in, but a carefully prepared *Business-funded* plan. The common IT budget for functions like human resources (HR), supply chain management (SCM), and finance is generally *distributed across the BUs* in some pre-agreed way (like revenue ratios), as in Table 6.10. Business-aligned IT organizations make it a habit of reporting the IT spends against the budget monthly to respective BUs. Since Technology spending directly impacts the bottom line, the last thing any BU wants is surprises on the IT spending front. In all BITA-driven organizations, *IT does not own the IT budget. Business does.* The overall spending against the *Business approved* budget is a vital measure of the monetary cost of IT to Business.

Table 6.10 Monetary costs: IT Budget

Business segment	BU Revenue	% of Ent Revenue	IT Projects	IT Infra & Ops	IT for Function Units	IT Common	IT Budget Estimate
			Direct BU Costs		Allocated BU Costs		
BU-A	120	35%	2.0	0.8	0.77	0.95	4.52
BU-B	68	20%	1.5	0.6	0.44	0.54	3.08
BU-C	152	45%	3.0	1.0	0.99	1.21	6.20
Function Units (Combined)	0		1.0	1.2			
IT Common (Opex + Capex)	0		1.2	1.5			
Enterprise	340		8.7	5.1			13.8

(All a mounts in USD Mn)
(*Allocation of Function Unit's IT budget is done here by distributing the FU budget across BUs in the same proportion as BU revenues, for example., 35% to BU-A)

In this case, the IT budget is $13.8 million for the year, which is the aggregation of the IT budget (direct + allocated) of the three business units. This works out to about 4 percent of the revenue, which for most industry segments is within the ballpark. For tech companies like telecom and software, the ratio of technology budget to revenues could be higher. The *monetary cost index* (MCI) is the difference between actual cost and budgeted cost, divided by the budgeted cost. Since costs *subtract* from the value, the MCI, like all other forms of cost, is ideally a negative quantity. The lower it is, the better. Let us say the measured expenditure on IT at the end of the year is $13.0 million. In this case,

MCI = (Actual cost − budgeted cost) / (budgeted cost), or (13.0 − 13.8) / 13.8. that is, − 0.06

In the case of nonmonetary cost factors, there is a much larger element of subjectivity due to which a direct computation is not feasible. The best way to determine the cost associated with these elements, viz effort, risk, and complexity, is to jointly develop a template to obtain perception-based feedback from multiple stakeholders on the various elements of effort, risk, and complexity of working with Technology, on a scale of 1 to 5. The average of the scores under each cost head across all respondents is computed to get the respective indices, as exemplified in Table 6.11:

^For example, the elements of *effort* by Business to avail IT services may be defined and scored as follows (average scores, 5 being most satisfactory):

BA/SPOC availability	5.0
Escalation matrix	4.6
Speedy response	4.6
Flexible policies	4.2
Average	**4.6**

Table 6.11 Nonmonetary IT costs

Attribute	Index Name	Scale (Max)	Average Score	Index Value*
Effort	ECI	5	4.6^	0.08
Risk	RCI	5	4.3	0.14
Complexity	XCI	5	4.0	0.20

Index value is computed as (Scale − Score)/ Scale.

Table 6.12 Composite cost index

Cost Component	Weight (%)	Score	Index
MCI (money)	40	–0.06	-0024
ECI (effort)	20	+0.08	+0.016
RCI (risk)	25	+0.14	+0.035
XCI (complexity)	15	+0.20	+0.030
Composite Cost Index (CCI)	100		**+0.057**

As the score is always less than or equal to the scale, the nonmonetary cost indexes are always positive (that is, they take *away* from the overall benefits to *reduce* the value), or at best zero. The above values are summarized in Table 6.12 and plotted in Figure 6.9.

The composite cost index is the sum of the *weighted* cost indexes. Our overall CCI here is +0.057. This quantity will be taken off the benefits index to arrive at the overall Business value of IT. As an Index, BVIT is commonly expressed as:

Composite BVIT Index = Composite Benefits Index – Composite Cost Index

In our sample case, composite benefits index is 0.820, and the composite cost index is 0.057. Therefore,

BVIT Index = 0.820 – 0.057 = 0.763.

The estimation of Business value of Technology (BVIT) is a useful means of assessing the role and contribution of Technology to Business in the Digital Age, though the specific method you choose to do so may

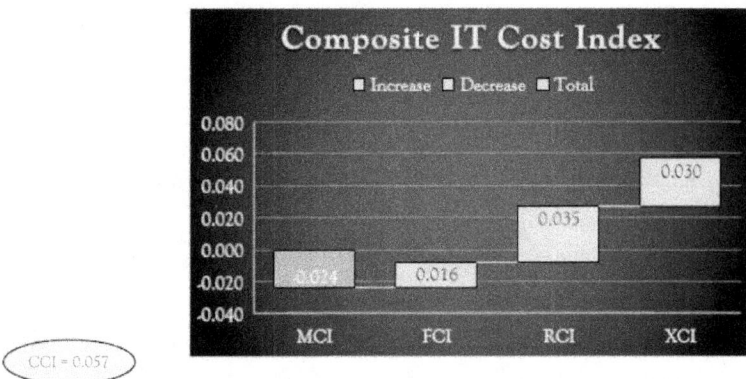

Figure 6.9 Composite IT cost index

not be exactly aligned with above sample process. The important thing is that both the benefits and the cost must be recognized as constituents of value. If you are targeting greater benefits, the cost is usually higher too, as life has taught us in all its walks.

There is no universal BVIT benchmark scale, but in general, a score above 0.65 is considered acceptable, though the more important thing is the *trend* seen over time. If you are moving steadily upward, it is a better sign than having a relatively higher score that is stagnating, or worse, plunging over time.

A lack of functional alignment between Business and Technology could lead to some of the following fallouts, which are among the root causes of business failure:

1. Unregulated dollar spend on Technology (IT) items
2. IT costs being an eternal enigma to the Business, often throwing up nasty surprises
3. Unsupportive IT policies, such as coercing stance on IT security and software usage
4. Digital divide within the enterprise (wide gap in technology adoption across functions)
5. Invisibility into IT performance, causing loss of sync between Business and IT
6. Building products/services that no one wants to buy
7. Launch of new products/services frequently delayed, leading to lost market share
8. Failure to execute or deliver on time, cost, schedule by IT, leading to lost credibility, delayed TTM
9. Insufficient adoption of social media and mobility for Business
10. Virtually nil instances of IT-led upsells
11. Archaic processes that have a constraining rather than liberating effect on Business
12. Missing or inadequate governance structure for Business–IT engagement.
13. Failure to execute on business-led technology initiatives (e.g. digital marketing campaign)

The question is, would you rather wait for some of these issues (among others) to show up *before* you institute systems to track BVIT, or be *proactive* in making BVIT measurement a part of your BITA strategy to *preempt* these?

Measuring BVIT is an effective way to gauge the ability of Business and Technology to create value together. It is not a rigid process, being amenable to construction according to the specific needs and priorities of an enterprise. You also do not have to wait for a "perfect" setting to initiate it. You can start small and build gradually to reach higher and higher levels of maturity. Several organizations have successfully taken the concept of BVIT measurement from concept to reality. BVIT is not only a barometer of functional alignment but also an excellent lead indicator of business outcomes along a wide range of parameters. Organizations that have institutionalized BVIT measurement are, therefore, much more likely to stay on track through improved preparation and timely course corrections. The important thing is to get started.

CHAPTER 7

The Tactical Touch

*"There is nothing so useless as doing efficiently
that which should not be done at all."*

Example 7.1

This is a story from the very nascent days of the computer age, somewhere in the early 1990s. Every computer then was a standalone universe unto itself, and the concept of networking was still unheard of outside the research and academic world. I was called to attend to a service problem in the minicomputer system at the remote plant of an industrial house. Getting to that place involved taking an overnight train to the nearest rail station, and from there if you were lucky, you got a cab, else you had to bus it to a point on the highway which was 6–7 km away from the plant, so the customer had to send a vehicle to pick you up from here. As this was before the mobile/e-mail era, precise coordination was vital. I arrived at the plant one early afternoon, ready to investigate the reported technical problem. As soon as I came in, I was escorted to the office of the plant manager who was apparently not big on small talk and came straight to the point: Did I come ready to deploy the operating system upgrade, which was necessary to run his new material-accounting software? I had no idea of this, and more to the point, their hardware was not supportive of the new operating system version that was being asked! Turned out that a fortnight ago, our sales manager had visited the plant and when he was apprised of the material accounting issue, he had promptly promised that he would get it fixed by upgrading to the new operating system during the next visit of "my engineer." Either the sales guy was blissfully unaware of the limitations of the systems he sold for a living, or he had just parachuted himself out when the going became turbulent; which I could fleetingly sympathize with because being at the receiving end of the plant manager's outburst I can imagine the situation would have been quite nasty for the sales manager.

The issue here is not just that I was caught unawares and subjected to rough treatment. In hindsight, it was perfectly understandable from the customer's point of view. Visits from vendors to this remote place were few and far between, so there were higher expectations from each visit. Plus, he felt let down by the company's unkept promises. It was bad enough that the sales manager gave false commitments. But not giving even a hint to prepare me for the situation was worse. This when we both worked out of the same office in Delhi, and our seats were just across the aisle from each other! Often, we even had lunch together! This incident led to a serious escalation to the customer's top management, and this being a national account, the senior management of our company also got involved. But with all the restoration efforts, the cracks in our credibility were never fully repaired.

To say that such incidents do not occur in today's era of digital business would be economizing with the truth. The style and form are now different since the channels of communication now permit only a behind-the-scenes interaction with customers for the most part. Whether it is the automated interactive voice response (IVR) or an executive interaction that set the expectation, your record of *delivering on promises* to your stakeholders defines you much more sharply than your mission statement, testimonials, or advertisements. The core issue is the *alignment* between Business and Technology to uphold the *credibility*, which is built not on promises made, but on *executing* on those promises.

Tactical alignment is about Business and Technology locking step for executing not just on the broad company strategy, but on all the explicit and implied promises to the customer at various moments of truth. In short, it is about *walking the talk*. In today's world of digital business, tactical alignment implies that Business and Technology are complementing each other in the execution of the digital strategy to deliver a superior experience to their customer *throughout the lifecycle*. An environment that promotes open communication to keep Business and Technology always in sync is critical to sustaining tactical alignment. The IT systems

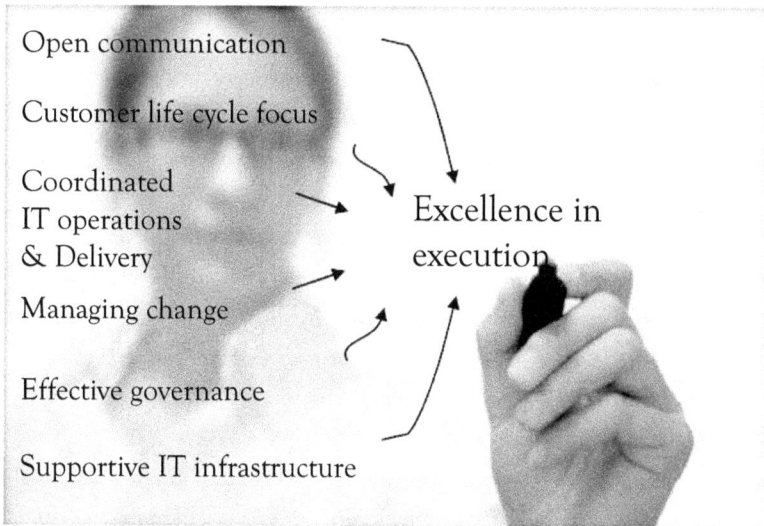

Figure 7.1 Excellence in execution

and infrastructure must be designed to consistently ensure an outstanding customer experience aligned with, or exceeding, the aspirations built through the various touch points. This means that Business is not only aware of Technology capabilities and limitations but is also willing to sponsor changes and enhancements in keeping with the rising customer expectations.

Some of the main contributors to excellence in execution are depicted in Figure 7.1. These are *qualitative* attributes, not given to precise measurement or the attainment of a *perfect* state. This means that irrespective of where you currently are on the execution curve, you can probably do it better. The following example will hopefully clarify this, by showing that complacency can be catastrophic.

Example 7.2

A global technology services company, which prided itself on its iron-clad processes, started its operations in India in 2009. The company was known for its keen attention to detail in planning their projects, leaving nothing to chance. The plans went through several layers of rigorous review before being approved for roll-out. To their prospective clients, the model gave a vivid impression of impeccability. Every conceivable process was boiler plated, and when an Indo-European venture signed them up as a strategic partner, it left no doubt in their mind that they were gaining an infallible ally.

And yet the first project that they co-executed for a telecom operator in India failed. The partner attributed this to not being in the groove with the cultural mores of the new environment, but no one was convinced that a reputed company would fail in its very first project in the country for such a reason. No one just enters a market without a thorough preassessment!

Too much rigidity of processes and policies is often at cross-purposes with the goals of tactical alignment. Intuition, anticipation, and discernment are some of the unwritten qualities that lead to successful execution. Instead of taking a spot decision to accommodate a minor request, if one must seek approval from someone far removed from the project, often in another continent, it's an open invitation to failure. The ability to think on your feet and the empowerment to decide and act are as essential to tactical alignment as your time-tested processes and policies.

To cut a long story short, it was a case of choosing process over perspicacity, and firmness over flexibility, that led to the debacle. When a minor change request was received, it was first resisted, and then reluctantly sent to the headquarters for "exception approval."

There was no proper local system of handling exceptions and escalations, probably because of the confidence in the efficacy of the templated processes. The cumulative effect of the processes was to block the realization of tactical goals.

Blind adherence and rigid stances, even when backed by time-tested processes and proven technology, are not conducive to successful execution. There is far too much dependence on things happening according to a script, which, as we have all learned—mostly the hard way—is a deceptive notion. Tactical alignment requires us to be inventive and *make* things happen *together*.

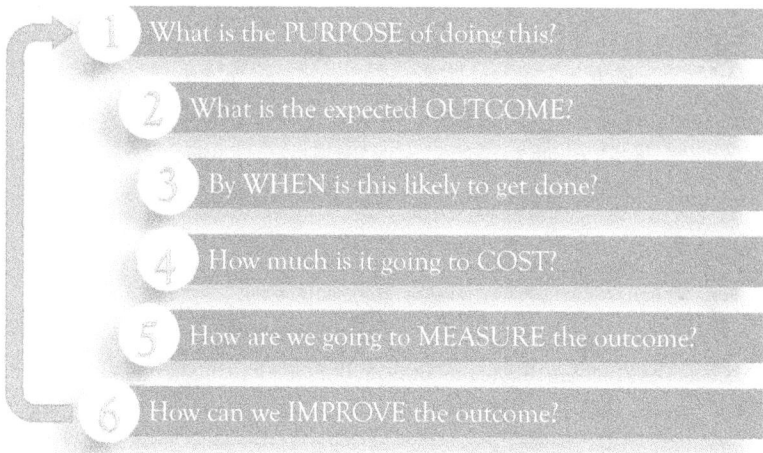

1. What is the PURPOSE of doing this?
2. What is the expected OUTCOME?
3. By WHEN is this likely to get done?
4. How much is it going to COST?
5. How are we going to MEASURE the outcome?
6. How can we IMPROVE the outcome?

Figure 7.2 Testing for tactical synchronization between Business and IT

Tactical alignment is the only dimension of BITA that is *visible* to your customers and other stakeholders. That is, *tactical alignment* is the fastest way to build perceptions about your company. Too many good practices and intentions have fallen by the wayside due to weak or missing tactical alignment. This may be avoided if Business and Technology are synchronized in their responses to the set of questions in Figure 7.2.[3]

These questions broadly apply to most tactical assignments like order fulfillment, service incident resolution, project delivery, and so on. They also apply to Change Requests that arise in the course of the assignment or project. I have found this simple questionnaire to be very useful in gauging tactical alignment. The question where I have seen the maximum divergence between Business and Technology is ironically not about the cost or schedule but on the expected *outcome* of the assignment. Strong formal and informal *communication* is essential to achieve synchronization. In the best BITA traditions, Business and Technology must achieve this harmony *before* the assignment. But sadly, in a rush to douse our daily fires, we ignore this, bringing our conflicts into the open—right in the customer's view. Also, notice that it is a *continuous* loop. After achieving the targeted outcome, Business and Technology agree on the way to improve the outcome, and the cycle gets repeated.

> **Exercise:** *Take any significant project or service that is being rendered by your company to a customer. Ask these six questions to concerned folks from Business and Technology and compare the answers. Was there agreement on all the answers? If not, which are the key areas of divergence between Business and Technology (You may run this for several assignments to confirm the diagnosis)? How can the gaps be minimized?*

If there is an agreement between Business and Technology to a fair extent on these six simple questions, the chances are that your customers view you in a positive light on your ability to deliver on promises made.

Tactical alignment is not restricted to certain pockets of the customer experience lifecycle. It must be embedded in *every* stage of the customer's interaction with the product or service provider. It is important to note here that while your tactical maneuvers are in the customer's line of sight, tactical *alignment* is constructed and tempered deep within the nucleus of the enterprise, emanating from its cultural core. From here, it radiates into a glow that reflects in every stage of the customer lifecycle (CLC).

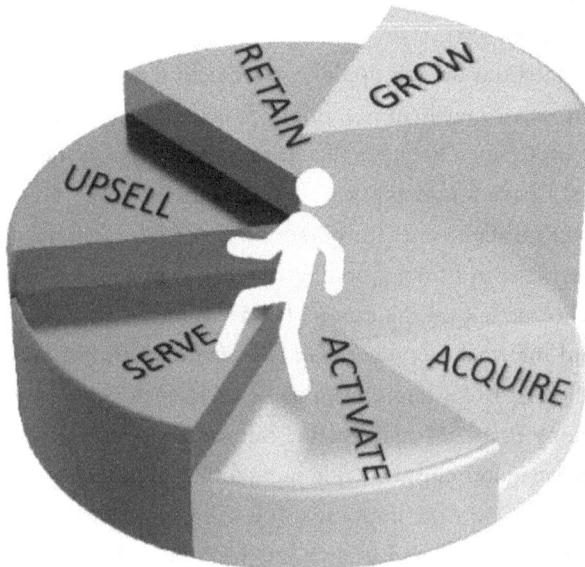

Figure 7.3 Customer Lifecycle (CLC) stages

The typical CLC stages are depicted in Figure 7.3. Your actions as a company at *each* of these steps are openly visible to your prospects and customers, and hence have a direct and considerable influence on building perceptions about your company. The only tool at your disposal for avoiding a misstep is tactical alignment between your Business and Technology functions, the importance of which grows in line with your transformation to a digital enterprise. The CLC steps are very steep and slippery, and tactical alignment is your handrail. Let us look at the salient features of each CLC stage, as it applies in the new age of digital business.

Table 7.1 CLC stages

	CLC Stage	Actions (examples)	Digital Drivers and Tactical Tools
1	Acquire	Lead generation and profiling	Marketing and promotions, Digital channels
		Customer inquiry (RFP) and response	Needs assessment, advocacy
		Sales communication and closure	Feasibility analysis, order logging
2	Activate	Order processing	Automated workflow, orchestration, ERP
		Allotment of services	Tool-based aggregation and provisioning
3	Serve	Order fulfillment	Delivery, customization, and activation
		Incident tracking and management	Customer experience management system
		Service response tracking and analysis	Voice-of-customer (VoC) and social media (SM) analytics
4	Upsell	Personalized offerings	Market segmentation, targeted campaigns
		Service/Product upgrades	Personalized offers, Cloud-based models
5	Retain	Customer analytics	Data mining and modeling, Big Data tools
		Loyalty management	Sentiment analytics, loyalty programs
6	Grow	New product/service (co-)development	Incremental, iterative, Agile cadence
		Customer advocacy, referrals	Trusted advisory, SM analytics, collaboration

> *Exercise:* List the actions under each CLC stage as applicable to your in-dustry. Which stages of CLC are Business and IT teams in your company not *perfectly* aligned in, and how is business value being eroded due to this? What steps must you take to align on these?

The essence of tactical alignment lies in the realization and demon-stration that Business and Technology are not bifurcated in their respon-sibilities toward executing on the expectations of their stakeholders at any stage of the lifecycle. Gone are the days when the Business (or sales) team would deceptively win an order, perform a "hand-over" to Technology (delivery) team, and then expect them to execute it somehow, while being an arm's length away from the action.

As market competition increases, so does the struggle to win business and with it, the propensity to overlook the execution angle. Sales folks often sermonize about how tough the market is and, therefore, the execu-tion teams are *expected* to accept the aberrations that resulted from over-commitment, and "find a way" to deliver. Many real estate developers, investment brokers, and travel agents among others have been known to promise the world to get your business, but when it comes to execution, it is a completely different set of people, who may be well-meaning but are just as flustered as you about how to handle your legitimate requests. The situation is not very different from enterprises in most other sectors. To be fair to the sales folks, it does indeed require exemplary courage to walk away from a hard-fought deal only because of forecasted risks in execution.

The flip side of the coin is just as sticky. If you accept the order, you are extending an open invitation to early dissonance among the three main participants of the customer lifecycle—business, technology, and customer. I have never seen a satisfactory end to a narrative that involved a dissonance between Business and Technology early in the customer life-cycle. With time, it only grows.

Obviously, the way out of this quandary is to harmonize the two. And this further underlines the role of BITA, particularly on the tactical dimension. Execution is a critical component of tactical alignment, but tactical alignment goes beyond pure execution. Business and Technology

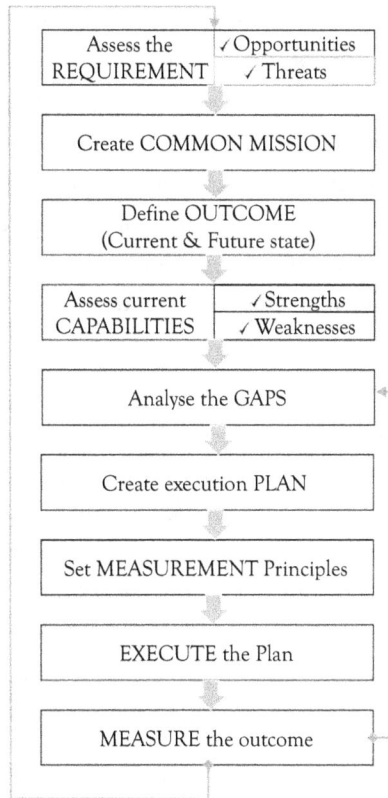

```
┌─────────────────────────────────────┐
│  Assess the      │ ✓ Opportunities   │
│  REQUIREMENT     │ ✓ Threats         │
└─────────────────────────────────────┘
              ↓
┌─────────────────────────────────────┐
│      Create COMMON MISSION           │
└─────────────────────────────────────┘
              ↓
┌─────────────────────────────────────┐
│      Define OUTCOME                  │
│      (Current & Future state)        │
└─────────────────────────────────────┘
              ↓
┌─────────────────────────────────────┐
│  Assess current  │ ✓ Strengths       │
│  CAPABILITIES    │ ✓ Weaknesses      │
└─────────────────────────────────────┘
              ↓
┌─────────────────────────────────────┐
│      Analyse the GAPS                │
└─────────────────────────────────────┘
              ↓
┌─────────────────────────────────────┐
│      Create execution PLAN           │
└─────────────────────────────────────┘
              ↓
┌─────────────────────────────────────┐
│      Set MEASUREMENT Principles      │
└─────────────────────────────────────┘
              ↓
┌─────────────────────────────────────┐
│      EXECUTE the Plan                │
└─────────────────────────────────────┘
              ↓
┌─────────────────────────────────────┐
│      MEASURE the outcome             │
└─────────────────────────────────────┘
```

Figure 7.4 Tactical alignment flowchart

must strive for harmony during the *buildup* to execution to assure consistency and predictability during the execution.

The simple flowchart in Figure 7.4 depicts the various steps required to be followed *in each CLC stage* for sustained tactical interlock. This may appear formidable at first, but over time, if BITA is working well in your organization, the essential elements will get ingrained in your methods as a natural course.

Tactical alignment is about being aware of and executing on commitments to customers (and other stakeholders) on behalf of the *organization*, irrespective of whether they were made by Business or Technology. To achieve tactical alignment, it is important to remember that the customer identifies you as the *company*, not as Technology or Business. That distinction ends at the gate of your office building.

Thus, tactical alignment can be assured only when Business and Technology are *fully aligned at every step* of the flowchart. The biggest problem in enterprises today is not the lack of a process for executing on these steps. The biggest problem is that the execution happens in silos. That is, the ownership of different steps of the flowchart is *either* with Business *or* with Technology, invisible to each other. This entails frequent hand-offs, in turn leading to gaps and slippages. These inevitably show up in the business performance, and companies spend a disproportionate amount of time trying to figure out what went wrong!

Exercise: *Let us go back to the six CLC steps we identified earlier: Acquire–Activate–Serve–Retain–Upsell–Grow. Apply the various steps in our tactical flowchart, top to bottom, to each of these stages successively. Can you identify the areas in your organization where (1) process does not exist at all, (2) process exists but in isolation (Business and Technology are not aligned), and (3) process exists and is in harmony (Business and Technology are well-aligned)?*

Our process/workflow here has been overgeneralized to cater to a broader sect. It is advisable that you spend some time to create a tactical flowchart best suited to *your* environment as a template for sequencing activities and determining pitfalls in execution, for *each* CLC stage.

Tactical Basics in the Digital Age

Let us now turn our attention to the digital world. It's a fast-expanding world, where the number of entities (applications, things, people) communicating among each other is growing exponentially, well beyond the human population. The separation between the cyber and the physical is diminishing rapidly, spawning new and unforeseen business models. New means, methods, and mechanisms are called into play to enable enterprises to deliver personalized experiences to their customers as an instrument of survival. The question is, how do Business and Technology leverage tactical alignment as a driver of enterprise growth in this altered landscape?

Well, here's the nub: The core principles of tactical alignment stay relevant in this digital world as well! All that has changed is the *tools*. When we look at the many tools at our fingertips today, it becomes difficult to imagine how business was ever conducted without these. *Digital technology platforms*, which enable a host of digital tools to be provisioned quickly for delivering personalized experiences, are the bedrock of tactical alignment in today's world. While having one-off digital features like tablet-based sales tracking system for the field force is a positive step, the real value is unlocked only when you can dynamically adapt and apply *diverse* digital tools in sync with the demands of the business. These demands may change rapidly and unpredictably. An attempt to develop and launch new tools from the ground up in response to every change would render you uncompetitive. A ready digital platform, on the other hand, enables quick creation, reconfiguration, and management of digital services and tools, and is thus your redeemer in the digital world.

A digital platform refers to the service-oriented apparatus for leveraging various digital technologies and their intersections among each other to create new business solutions. The *digital technology platform* allows for development and delivery of digital *services* in the form of *reusable building blocks* by leveraging an array of component technologies, isolating the Business

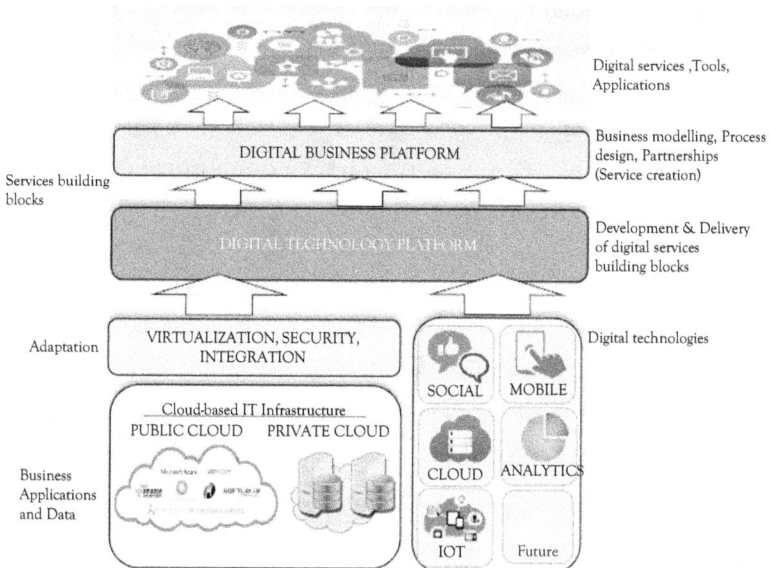

Figure 7.5 Digital technology platform model

from downstream complexities. The creation of personalized offers/plans and dynamic reconfigurations of process workflows to suit new business requirements are among the operations that happen at the *digital business platform*, using the services provided by the digital technology platform as building blocks. Together, the digital technology platform and the digital business platform constitute the all-important *digital platform*. A digital platform allows enterprises to reap business benefits by speeding up the delivery of new digital services, leveraging social media, enterprise mobility, Cloud computing, Big data analytics, and Internet of Things (IoT), among others.

A functioning digital platform meets the challenges associated with the launch and operation of digital services a lot more efficiently to deliver a unique tactical advantage. The following advantages make a compelling case for its implementation:

1. It increases the range of solutions by leveraging intersections between technologies.
2. It facilitates quick construction and configuration of Business services using standard components and interfaces.
3. It facilitates standardization of digital architecture (SOA).
4. It offers interoperability with other digital platforms.
5. It supports solutions using components from different vendors.
6. It accelerates the digital delivery process.

In simpler, more businesslike terms, the cumulative advantages delivered by a digital platform, emanating from a combination of the above technical advantages, include the following:

- Creation of new revenue opportunities (expansion)
- Reduction in time to market—faster product/service development cycle (acceleration)
- Personalized offerings leading to enhanced customer experience (personalization)
- Reduced long-term cost due to a common platform for multiple services (standardization)
- Engagement of customers and partners in devising solutions (collaboration)

These are, of course, tactical matters whose achievement in the Digital Age is a function of two critical attributes that were almost nonexistent in the analog era: *Adoption of digital technologies for business*, and *alignment of Technology with Business*. Enterprises that embrace these in their tactics as best practices are the undisputed leaders in their domains today.

Enterprises that have adopted the digital platform early have a clear edge in terms of speed and efficacy of operations over their more complacent rivals who await the next big thing (or worse, a catastrophe) to embark on this journey. Adopting a digital platform in gradual but definite stages in line with the digital maturity of the enterprise is an important step to tactical alignment in the digital world.

> ***Exercise:*** *Can you identify the discrete digital tools and technologies in use for achieving the business outcomes listed above, in your enterprise?*

The schematic of the digital platform shown in Figure 7.5 is purely at a conceptual level. In any case, there is no standard topology that would apply in every situation, though there is some work in progress to standardize the digital *architectures*. However, it is the nailing down of the *details* that makes execution efficient and predictable. As everyone is not a technologist, the best approach is to use the conceptual framework for seeking consensus and approval, and then give the reins to the technologists to assess, build, integrate, and test the required components to implement your digital platform as a project steered by stakeholders from both Technology and Business management functions.

A good question to ask at this juncture would be: What is the relevance of the digital platform to our discussion on the *tactical alignment* between Business and Technology? Well, the simple answer is that diverse but *disconnected* digital technologies working in isolation cannot lead to tactical alignment and create business value for the enterprise, as demonstrated in countless situations from across industries.

Example 7.3

At a board-level meeting of a book publishing company, a decision was taken to deliver a selection of books in the soft version, that is, download-able by the user on devices like Kindle. Of course, this is an inevitability that every book publisher is faced with to survive in today's world. Models have evolved to deliver the books through online retailers (like Amazon) directly to user-owned devices. The online versions are, of course, available at a lower price than the paperbacks and hardcovers. Yet, since the "pro-duction" costs are very marginal, it is a profitable venture. The big worry for publishers, of course, is piracy, which erodes margins and eventually renders the model unsustainable. The said publisher created an Online Books Division (OBD) in their company, responsible for the management (including antipiracy measures) and sale of e-books. They set up a secure link for their e-books to be accessed through online retailers' portals, ena-bling customers to browse, select, order, pay for, and acquire the products of their choice.

Now, the book business is heavily dependent on user feedback. Some books become best-sellers while others just languish on bookshelves. Publish-ers and authors depend heavily on qualitative feedback. Another division of the company, let's call it the User Contact Group (UCG), ran appli-cations where a registered reader (reviewer) could independently upload comments for a book of a given genre. These apps were mobile-enabled, storing user information and feedback on a public cloud set up by UCG. To gauge sentiments from social media and understand reader preferences, UCG had shown a great deal of foresight to set up a Data Analytics center. The company identified clear demographic markers and used the analysis to segregate books according to user feedback.

It was clear that this company was serious about using technology for business. It made the right moves and spent a good deal of resources on technology adoption. But there was a problem: In spite of some excellent feedbacks from reviewers, sales did not pick up, and hardly any book from this publisher made it to the top-100 list in any category through the year. Clearly, the company had failed to sense the user pulse and position its products right.

On deep diving into the root causes, it was discovered that while OBD and UCG were working well independently, they were separate islands with no bridge between them. Feedback was received at UCG through many channels spread across the world, but there was no way available for OBD to channelize the promotions according to the consolidated feedback from readers. Thus, wrong books were often overpromoted, and the good ones left unsung! This impacted not only the business but the credibility of the publisher. As another disturbing fallout, the company witnessed a spike in online piracy. When you know your aces, you take increased precautions to guard them. When you do not, your guard gets inadvertently lower.

A friend from the publishing world narrated this story, and I may be missing some details. However, the point is that the best digital technologies will fail in their mission if they are unable to work across functional boundaries. This is where a digital platform comes in as an indispensable tactical tool to enable efficient usage and synergies across multiple technologies, functions, and processes.

Tactics are a function of your strategy. They are the steps to execute your strategy. Thus, there can be no tactical plan without a strategy in place. A digital platform embodies your digital strategy and thus provides the blueprint for tactical alignment.

How do you measure tactical alignment? It may neither be possible nor required to reduce tactical alignment to a precise number. In the chapter on functional alignment, we discussed how the benefits of Technology to Business could be tracked using several indices. These functional indices are also a good measure of the *tactical* alignment between Business and Technology. In any case, tracking too many different parameters across various dimensions of BITA could fast become an overhead, outweighing the potential benefits. The attempt, therefore, is to unify measurement to the extent possible.

While we may track the same parameters as functional alignment to gauge tactical alignment, there are a couple of subtle differences.

First, tactical alignment is primarily related to *trends*, rather than absolute measures. An upward trend on any of the measurement parameters is indicative of a positive tactical alignment between Business and

Technology on that parameter. A *downward* trend, on the other hand, even if the absolute score is in the top bracket, is a signal of weakening of the tactical bond between Business and Technology.

Second, tactical alignment has a strong *qualitative* component, which cannot be measured but must be assessed. It depends on the spirit of trust between Business and Technology, how their actions and intentions are perceived by customers and other stakeholders, their credibility in terms of meeting commitments, the synchronicity of their communication and follow-through, and so on. The best way to assess this is to periodically ask a set of relevant questions to test the alignment.

With the enhancement of Business value being the aim, it is best that the questions to qualitatively assess tactical alignment are organized along the business value of IT (BVIT) axes, viz., customer engagement, service excellence, economic contribution, and technological readiness, as discussed below.

Customer Engagement: Customer engagement is the key to long-term competitive advantage, being the primary driver of customer loyalty and hence sustained market leadership through positive references. Many progressive enterprises are discovering the value of engaging customers even before the sell–deliver–care cycle, by seeking participation in research, prototypes, and pilots. Customer experience management systems are ruling the roost in a growing number of enterprises, tracking each interaction through the lifecycle. Digital technologies like Big data have effectively helped enterprises to reach the bottom of the pyramid and define systems to measure experience parameters at different stages of the customer's lifecycle, and then correlate them for delivering personalized support. These programs are all aimed at achieving one tactical outcome: increased customer engagement. Comprehensive tactical alignment requires that the facilitators for these programs are deeply ingrained in the enterprise.

Measuring and tracking customer engagement, both quantitatively and qualitatively, as a shared responsibility of both Business and Technology is a key determinant of business value creation in the digital economy.

If you are unable to relate to your customers' progressive expectations and experiences at every stage of the lifecycle, you clearly do *not* have your finger on the customer's pulse. You would do well to prepare an action plan and an assessment methodology as your foremost priority.

Here are a few sample questions for qualitative assessment of tactical alignment on the customer engagement parameter. The *equivalence* in the response from Business and Technology is the determinant of tactical alignment between Business and Technology.

1	Which activities are associated with each stage of the CLC [acquire to grow] in your enterprise?
2	Of the above, which are the top three contributors to (potential) disengagement of customers?
3	What actions would prevent customers from disengaging with the enterprise?
4	What are the three significant changes in customers' expectations from your enterprise in the last two years?
5	What are the steps taken by your company to meet these changing expectations?

Like with other tactical attributes, these questions must be posed separately to Business and Technology. If the answers are comparable, it is a sign of good tactical alignment for that attribute.

Delivery Efficiency: Delivery efficiency has the advantage that it lends itself to more credible quantitative measurement than customer engagement. Its tactical relevance is high, however, as it directly impacts several attributes of business and customer value creation. In general, delivery efficiency affects the following business attributes (the term "product" here refers to both product and *service* offerings to customers):

- Product features and performance (differentiation)
- Product quality
- Time-to-market
- Standards conformance and interoperability
- Scalability and upgradability
- Extracting maximum value from IT spending

Each of these attributes is a feature of the tactical landscape. A failure to rise to your stakeholders' expectations on any of the above characteristics could well be rooted in tactical misalignment between Business and Technology. Of course, your culture, strategy, structure, and spirit of innovation, among others play a part in customer value creation, but they only set the stage for the *tactical show* in which Business and Technology are the lead performers. Like with any concert, it is not just the individual performances but the on- and off-stage chemistry between the leads that raises the level of enthrallment. That chemistry is called alignment.

A qualitative assessment is essential to ascertain any potential gaps between perception and measurement, even where numeric analysis is straightforward—as with delivery efficiency index. Apart from regular BVIT monitoring of DEI trends as determinants of tactical alignment, therefore, some *critical questions* need to be asked to test for Business and Technology being on a common platform qualitatively. These could include the following.

1	How is change *management* handled? What are the various tools/stages involved?
2	Which stages of the delivery cycle (Requirements to Production) are the biggest bottlenecks to efficient and timely delivery?
3	What are the steps required to eliminate or minimize these bottlenecks?
4	How is the final user acceptance testing (UAT) of the solution developed for the market/customer performed?
5	How are Business and IT kept in sync on delivery related issues like slippages, scope changes, and cost overruns?

Again, the important point here is that both Business and Technology, having equal stakes in delivery, are in agreement on the responses to the questions such as above.

Operational Health: Operations are the most visible aspect of tactics. In fact, it is often considered synonymous with tactics. Before the digital era, operations (like support and maintenance) were primarily seen as a tedious but necessary overhead of the business. The digital era has shifted this from an overhead to an opportunity for gaining competitive advantage. In our context, if delivery is concerned with *change*, operations are what keeps the business *running*. A series of internal and external practices make up the operations universe of the enterprise, as we discussed in the chapter on functional alignment. These practices are aimed at the attainment of some critical business outcomes, which include the following.

- Fulfillment of the customer order (commissioning, configuration, etc.)
- Uninterrupted availability of Business and Operations support systems
- Efficient incident management (service restoration, problem resolution)
- Confidentiality, integrity, and availability of critical data (security and privacy)
- Disaster recovery and business continuity

The operations health index (OHI) is a good barometer of operational efficacy (functional alignment) while its *trend* over time is an indicator of tactical alignment. The Digital Age is an era of *Business-outcome* driven Technology (IT) operations.[3] Therefore, alignment between Business and Technology on the operational axis is one of the most critical success factors for Business. Enterprises where operations are exclusively in the purview of Technology (IT) often get left behind in the relentless race and often fail to reach their aspiration of becoming successful digital enterprises.

Here too, apart from regular *OHI measurement* as a dipstick for operational health, it is essential that Business and Technology are aligned with each other in their responses to some qualitative questions, which could include the following:

1	Which operational parameters are being regularly tracked to monitor your business performance?
2	What are the major operational drawbacks responsible for suboptimal outcomes?
3	What is preventing your customer-facing teams from consistently meeting customer SLAs?
4	What are the top three to five actions required to overcome the problems found in Q3?
5	How do (or can) IT operations contribute to giving a differentiating edge to your business?

Economic Contribution: The role of tactical alignment in direct economic contribution is best assessed by revisiting our definition of Technology. As we have said at several points in this book, Technology is not just the faceless, back-end entity entrusted with fixing technical problems. It has a much broader charter, encompassing presales technical consultants, business analysts, system architects, project delivery and operations teams, technical specialists, and information security officers, among other allied roles. The question is, in this era of technology dominance in business, can a company afford to ignore the combined potential of this invaluable resource pool to boost its economic performance? Structures and silos are often the biggest bottlenecks in leveraging the full potential, and the first tactical step is to loosen them. Forget about the dangers of "stepping on each other's toes" and focus on enhancing economic contribution as your primary purpose. Economic contribution is an outcome that results from Business and Technology working *jointly* on the following tactical endeavors:

- Generation of opportunities, leads, and prospects
- Responding to business queries, Requests for Proposals/Information
- Market/customer requirements analysis
- Creating winning business proposals
- Value demonstrations, for example, proof of concept (POC)/ proof of value (POV)
- Technical discussions and follow-through
- Closure and contracting
- Reference generation and upselling
- Creating an enabling environment—Sales automation (SFDC), mobility, and so on.

When we discussed the economic contribution index in the context of functional alignment, we touched upon the direct and indirect contribution by Technology to Business. As in the case of other tactical attributes, the numeric score here must be supplemented with a qualitative assessment to get a grip on the tactical alignment. However, I would put a higher weight on the numeric score here since this is ultimately about revenue and profitability. Nevertheless, some qualitative analysis would help determine if *both* Business and Technology are invested in economic value creation and if there is potential for upscaling. Business and Technology team members' comparable response to the following sample questions will help ascertain this.

1	What are the different stages of the selling cycle in your organization?
2	In what ways *can* IT (in your organization) contribute to business generation? <refer CLC>
3	In what ways *does* IT (in your organization) contribute to business generation?
4	What are the biggest reasons for the gap between (2) and (3)?
5	What are the required steps for filling these gaps to generate enhanced revenues in next FY?

A set of questions for qualitative assessment on this parameter is possible for every environment. A combination of absolute ECI score, ECI trends, and qualitative assessment could be a potent mix for realizing your full economic potential as a digital enterprise.

Technology readiness: Unlike economic contribution where results speak for themselves, the assessment of the tactical angle in *technology readiness* takes us into nebulous territory. How do you gauge the extent of Technology-readiness, that is, whether it is *enough*, or if it is *right* for your enterprise? Is a company using fiber MPLS ring for interoffice connectivity, or deploying state-of-the-art telepresence system, higher on the tech-readiness scale than a company which allows its employees to access the company intranet from their mobile devices? There is no fixed answer. The tactical alignment on the tech-readiness front is predicated not on how much or which technology is adopted, but on the spirit of trusted advisory and collaboration that precedes and accompanies the adoption and use of technology for business.

Tactical alignment here begins with Technology (IT) continually scanning the market landscape and advising Business on the right technologies to navigate that landscape. In far too many companies, Business charts the company's technological path independently while Technology (IT) is only an implementer. That won't work for digital enterprises. The role of Technology is of chief navigator through the complex technological maze that surrounds the enterprise. Tactical alignment here refers to Business and Technology having agreement on the appropriate technologies for business, and the process of their assimilation in the enterprise environment.

In the chapter on functional alignment we studied an elaborate method of determining the technology adoption index. However, a degree of qualitative assessment is required to complete the tactical perspective too. Here are some sample questions on which Business and Technology must show agreement to demonstrate tactical alignment on the tech-readiness attribute.

1	Which technologies do you consider most important for your business today?
2	What are the key reasons for the failure to adopt all the required technologies in your enterprise?
3	Which technologies are deployed in your enterprise but not fully leveraged for business?
4	Which critical areas of your business could be improved with the adoption of newer technologies?
5	Which technologies do you recommend for phasing out due to lost relevance or newer versions?

Adoption of the right technologies driven by a robust BITA is one of the defining aspects of digital transformation and ultimately, your emergence as a successful digital enterprise. The good news is, you already have the potential to achieve this within your enterprise. It only must be unlocked.

Before we leave the topic, a few words on the roadblocks to tactical alignment. Some of the main inhibitors to tactical alignment between Business and Technology are indicated in Table 7.2. Some are rooted in antiquated practices, and others in rigid mindsets. With some effort, however, these can be overcome, yielding positive change.

Tactical alignment does not happen in a flash. It evolves. And during the evolution, many inhibitors may block your path. As you move toward your vision in this backdrop, it is natural to miss your step occasionally. That's OK, if you picked up a tip or two from the experience. I am reminded here of a phrase from the famous HBO series, *Westworld*: "*Evolution forged the entire sentient life on this planet using only one tool—the mistake.*" The message is, every time you falter, you learn (evolve) and this helps to adapt better.

Taken together, the seven dimensions of Business–Technology alignment create the platform on which the successful digital enterprise stands. As we have emphasized in this book, technology plays the lead role in digital transformation, but it is not a substitute for the *other* necessary ingredients in the digital cocktail. Technical superiority undoubtedly lends you an edge, but on its own cannot make you the frontrunner in the race to capitalize on the opportunities opened by the digital economy.

Table 7.2 Tactical alignment inhibitors

1	Insufficient formal and informal *communication*
2	Technology lacks *knowledge of the business challenges*
3	Business lacks *knowledge of Technology capabilities*
4	Business does not have *confidence in Technology*
5	Technology is a pure *back-end function* (at least in the view of Business)
6	Poor *Technology leadership*, lacking influencing capabilities
7	Misaligned *strategic priorities*
8	*Tight KRAs* leaving no flexibility with individuals ["not my job"]
9	*Budget inadequacy* leading to failure to acquire/build the right tools
10	Antiquated *IT infrastructure*, inhibiting the evolution of the *digital platform*
11	Lack of alignment at the level of *senior Business and Technology management*
12	Absence of a shared *sense of urgency* toward business priorities
13	Complex *Technology organization structure*, buck-passing
14	Organizational *silos*
15	Lack of *empowerment* of the frontline
16	Lack of *initiative* (read lack of *motivation*)
17	*Inertia* (resistance to change)
18	Inadequate *partnerships/alliances* (gaps in the value chain)

The torchbearers of the digital economy are enterprises that have not only adopted *digital technology* for business but also excelled on the *seven dimensions of BITA*. The combination imparts a winning edge that is hard to beat. Check this out for yourself. Think of the many businesses that are trying to make their way through the digital ocean. While many struggle to stay afloat, some clearly stand out—the winds and the waves only making them stronger. What is it that sets them apart?

If we could develop a scale for measuring an enterprise's progress in this Digital Age, I would vote that it is a function of the extent to which the combination of *digital technology* and *BITA dimensions* is harnessed for meeting its business needs.

The individual dimensional scores for your enterprise may be computed using the BITA calculator introduced in my book *Aligning Technology and Business for Digital Transformation*.[3] (Consider these as sample scores for now. The BITA calculator is also available on www.aligned-towin.com.) Using these scores, we could assign a *type number* to a digital

FOCUS ON TECHNOLOGY

DIGITAL TECHNOLOGY ADOPTION

BUSINESS-IT ALIGNMENT AT THE LEVEL OF

- CULTURE
- STRATEGY
- STRUCTURE
- PROCEDURE
- INTELLECT
- FUNCTION
- TACTICS

THE WINNING EDGE

- Improved speed to market
- More efficient development
- Improved change management
- Increased agility, iterative dev cycle
- Wider inter-operability
- Improved response to mkt changes
- Dynamic business modeling
- Greater value thru focused solutions
- Personalization
- Wider reach and accessibility
- Better customer engagement
- Improved CLM
- Higher predictability: cost, outcome
- Reduced risk
- Better quality: Continuous Impr.
- Superior execution
- Measurement of business value
- Improved employee morale
- Culture of Innovation
- Greater economic value creation

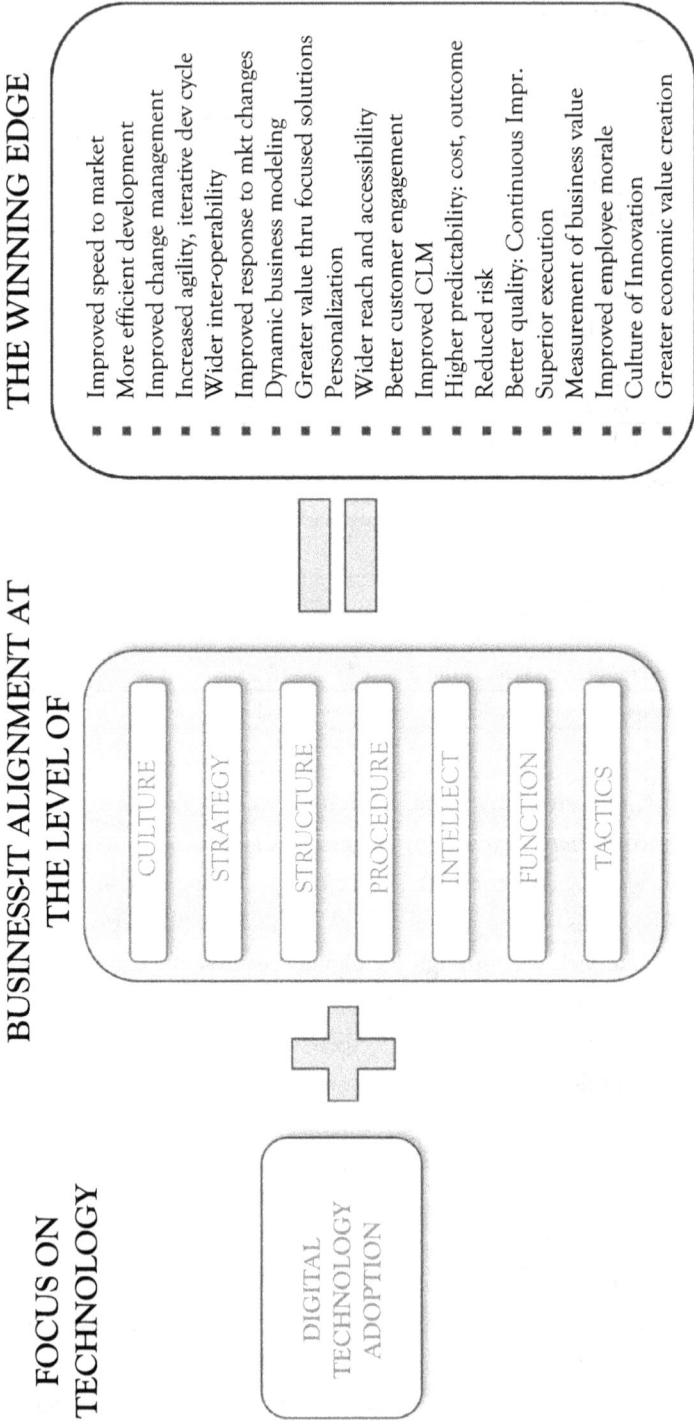

Figure 7.6 The winning edge

enterprise, as explained below. The higher the type number, the more evolved is the enterprise on the BITA scale.

Set a reasonably high but attainable target score for each of the eight attributes in Table 7.3. To start with, *0.50* is a good target for all attributes, though you are free to set *different* targets for each attribute. Now, for each attribute that you have scored *at least* the target, increase your type by one. In the given sample, you are clearly a type 3 digital enterprise. You may review it each year and recheck your type. While determining your type, your target on *technology adoption* must *always* be achieved. Thus, if you have exceeded the cutoff (0.50 here) for technology adoption and two other dimensions, you are type 3 (as in the example). However, if you have crossed the cutoff on four dimensions, but your technology adoption score is less than the cutoff, you are still Type 0. By the way, many companies start off their digital journeys as Type 0, so no need for alarm! The aim must be to keep progressing.

Table 7.3 Sample dimensional scores

Tech Adoption	Culture	Strategy	Structure	Process	Intellect	Function	Tactics
0.57	0.55	0.44	0.56	0.24	0.36	0.21	0.28

The digital economy is predicted to gross over $1 trillion by 2022. The aptitudes we have discussed in this book are among its primary drivers. These are going to be decisive in determining who wins and who falls by the wayside. Would you not make some simple investments in the right direction to acquire them *now*, rather than scamper to make course corrections later?

This book aimed to emphasize the need to embrace the seven dimensions of Business Technology alignment for taking advantage of the digital opportunity. Individuals and enterprises who have adopted BITA as an instrument of value creation clearly have the winning edge in the digital economy. The understanding of BITA and its infusion in the cultural, strategic, structural, procedural, intellectual, functional, and tactical streams of the enterprise is, therefore, a matter of critical importance for a digital enterprise. The good news is that assimilation of BITA does not call for new skills to be acquired or concepts to be learned. It is just the application of principles and practices that we are already familiar with through our experiences and aptitude. The various views, examples, stories, and exercises presented in the book will, I hope, rekindle these to give shape to your aspirations as an individual and your vision as an enterprise.

Acronyms

AI	Artificial Intelligence
API	Application Programming Interface
App	Application
B2B	Business-to-Business
B2C	Business-to-Consumer
BA	Business Analyst
BCI	Brain–Computer Interface
BFSI	Banking, Financial Services, and Insurance
BI	Business Intelligence
BITA	Business–IT Alignment, or Business–Technology Alignment
BPM	Business Process Management
BR	Business Requirement
BRS	Business Requirements Specifications
BSC	Balanced Score Card
BVIT	Business Value of IT
BYOD	Bring Your Own Device
CBI	Composite Benefits Index
CCI	Composite Cost Index
CDO	Chief Digital Officer
CDR	Call Data Record
CEM	Customer Experience Management
CEI	Customer Engagement index
CEO	Chief Executive Officer
CIO	Chief Information Officer
CLC	Customer Lifecycle
CLM	Customer Lifecycle Management
CM	Configuration Manager
CMI	Continuous Measurable Improvement
CMM	Capability Maturity Model
CMO	Chief Marketing Officer

COO	Chief Operating Officer
COTS	Commercial Off-the-Shelf
CPU	Central Processing Unit
CR	Change Request
CRM	Customer Relationship Management
C-SAT	Customer Satisfaction
CSI	Consulting and Systems Integration
CSP	Cloud Service Provider
CTO	Chief Technology Officer
DAL	Desired Attributed List [for Culture Dashboard]
DBA	Database Administrator
DEI	Delivery Efficiency index
DG	Diesel Generator
DR	Disaster Recovery
D-R	Direct Reports
e2e	End-to-end
EAI	Enterprise Application Integration
ECI	Economic-contribution index
EOY	End of Year
ERP	Enterprise Resource Planning
FCI	EFfort–Cost Index
FMS	Facility Management System
GPS	Global Positioning System
GRC	Governance, Risk, and Control
GTM	Go-to-Market
HCM	Human Capital Management
HD	High Definition
HNI	High Net-worth Individual
HR	Human Resources
HTML	Hyper-Text Markup Language
HTTP	Hyper-Text Transfer Protocol
HVAC	Heating, Ventilation, and Air Conditioning
IA	Impact Analysis
IaaS	Infrastructure-as-a-Service
IC	Integrated Circuit

ICT	Information and Communication Technology
IM	Integration Manager
IoT	Internet of Things
IP	Internet Protocol
IS	Information Security
IT	Information Technology
IVR	Interactive Voice Response
JD	Job description
KM	Knowledge Management
KMO	Knowledge Management Office
KPI	Key Performance Indicator
KRA	Key Result Area
KSO	Key Strategic Objective
LAN	Local Area Network
LOB	Line of Business
M2M	Machine-to-Machine
MCI	Monetary-Cost index
MIS	Management Information Systems
MPLS	Multi-Protocol Label Switching
NEP	Network Equipment Provider
NOTA	None of the above
ODC	Offshore Delivery (or Development) Center
OEM	Original Equipment Manufacturer
OHI	Operations-health index
OHP	Overhead Projector
OLS	Order Logging System
Opex	Operational Expense
P&L	Profit and Loss
PaaS	Platform-as-a-Service
PAT	Profit After Tax
PBT	Profit Before Tax
PI	Preconceived Idea
PMO	Program Management Office
PMP	Project Management Professional
PO	Purchase Order

POC	Proof of Concept
POV	Proof of Value
R&D	Research and Development
RCI	Risk-Cost index
RFP	Request For Proposal
RIM	Remote Infrastructure Management
RM	Release Manager
RoI	Return on Investment
SA	Solution Architect
SaaS	Software-as-a-Service
SBU	Strategic Business Unit
SC	Solution Consultant
SCM	Supply Chain Management
SLA	Service Level Agreement
SM	Social Media
SMAC	Social, Mobility, Analytics, and Cloud
SMART	Specific, Measurable, Achievable, Relevant, and Time-bound
SME	Small and Medium Enterprises
SOA	Service Oriented Architecture
SOP	Standard Operating Procedure
SPOC	Single Point of Contact
SR	Service Request
T&Q	Testing and Quality
TA	Tool Administrator
TAI	Technology-adoption index
TAT	Turn-Around Time
TBO	Think, Build, Operate
TCQ	Time, Cost, Quality
TOGAF	The Open Group Architecture Forum
TSP	Telecom Service Provider
TTM	Time-to-Market
UAT	User Acceptance Testing
XCI	Complexity-cost index
Y2K	Year 2000

Glossary of Terms

TERM	DEFINITION
.NET	Microsoft software-application development platform (Windows-based) supporting language interoperability
Agile development	a set of methods and practices where solutions evolve through collaboration between cross-functional teams
Analog	the opposite of digital. Any technology that doesn't break everything down into binary (digital) code to work is analog
Analytics	the discovery, interpretation, and communication of meaningful patterns in data
APIs	a set of instructions and standards that allows two software programs to communicate with each other
Application server	software that allows development, hosting, and rendering of web-based applications to users (clients)
Architecture (IT)	the overall design of a computing system's hardware, software, and protocols, and their logical and physical interrelationships
Authentication	the process of identifying an individual, based on a username and password, or biometric techniques
Bandwidth	the amount of data that can be transmitted in a fixed amount of time, or range within a band of frequencies or wavelengths
Big data	structured or unstructured data that organizations can potentially mine and analyze for business gains, characterized by high volume, velocity, and variety
Big data Analytics	the process of examining large amounts of data to uncover hidden patterns, correlations, and other insights
BITA Calculator	a simple assessment tool for estimating your BITA score. Also referred as BITA tool
Blockchain	a digitized, decentralized, public ledger of all crypto currency (e.g., Bitcoin) transactions
C++, Java	general-purpose, object-oriented programming languages
Call Data Record	a record that contains data fields which describe a specific instance of a telecommunication transaction
Capex	Capital expense, or funds used by a company to acquire, upgrade, and maintain physical assets
Central Processing System	the brain of a computer, which processes all the instructions given to it. Also referred as CPU

Churn	a measure of the number of individuals or items moving out of a collective group over a specific period
Client	system that rely on servers for processing power
Cloud	a distinct IT environment used for remotely delivering computing services-servers, storage, databases, networking, software
Compatibility	the capacity for two systems to work together without having to be altered to do so
Cookies	small files sent by a website to a user's computer to hold a modest amount of data specific to a user and website
Data center	a facility that centralizes an organization's IT operations and equipment
Data Communication Network	an interconnected system of computing devices capable of exchanging digital data amongst them
Data mining	the process of sorting through large data sets to identify patterns and establish relationships to solve problems
Data probe	devices or programs for retrieving data from the environment for analysis of its type, pattern, and trends
Data science	an interdisciplinary field about scientific methods, processes, and systems to extract knowledge or insights from data
Data Visualization	the technique used to convey information by encoding it as visual objects, like patterns and graphs
Data Warehouse	central repository constructed by integrating data from multiple heterogeneous sources
Data-Processing	the collection and manipulation of items of data to produce meaningful information
Digital divide	an inequality relating to access, use, or impact of ICT
Digitization	the process of converting information into a digital (computer-readable) format, in which the information is organized into bits
e-Commerce	general term for commercial activity over the Internet using B2B, B2C, or B2B2C modes
Encryption	the process of encoding a message or information in such a way that only authorized parties can access it
Engineering	projects delivery unit or organization, e.g., in a software company
Enterprise Mobility	focus on managing mobile devices, wireless networks, and other mobile computing services in a business context
Firewall	network security system to monitor and control incoming and outgoing traffic based on predefined rules
Gateway	a protocol converter used for linking networks or elements which use different protocols

Host	a computer on a network running server and client applications
Instant Messaging	online conversations involving real-time exchange of information over the Internet
intranet	a private network that is contained within an enterprise
IP-based	a system that uses the set of standards which ensure transmission and routing of data packets over the Internet
IPv6	the most recent version of the Internet Protocol, for identification and location of computers on networks. Replaces Ipv4
Iterative development	breaking down the software development of a large application into smaller chunks and repeated cycles
Kardashev scale	method of measuring a civilization's technological advancement
Machine learning (ML)	the science of getting computers to act by learning instead of being explicitly programmed to do the task
Mainframe	a high-performance computer used for large-scale computing purposes that require greater availability and security
Microprocessor	an integrated circuit (IC) which incorporates core functions of a computer's central processing unit (CPU)
Minicomputer	a computer that is intermediate between a microcomputer and a mainframe in size, speed, and capacity
MPLS	(multi-protocol label switching) a data carrying technique for terrestrial high-speed telecommunications networks
Multi-factor security	security system that requires more than one form of authentication to verify the legitimacy of a transaction
Network	communication fabric for allowing nodes (clients and servers) to share resources
Object-oriented	a programming model based on the attributes of objects rather than actions, and data rather than logic
Operating System	software that interacts with and manages computer hardware and allows the programs to run
Opex	Operational expense, or ongoing cost of running a product, business, or system.
Platform (architecture)	the foundation of hardware and software on which enterprise applications are built
Plug-and-play	the discovery and use of a hardware component without the need for manual device configuration or user intervention
Portal	a website that brings information from diverse sources, like e-mails, online forums, and search engines, together seamlessly
Real-time	a level of computer (or network) responsiveness that a user senses as instantaneous

Reuse	use of pre-developed blocks of software in current development to optimize development effort
Scalability	the capability of a system to handle a growing amount of work, or its potential to be enlarged to accommodate that growth
Segmentation	the process of dividing a broad consumer market into sub-groups of consumers based on some shared characteristics
Server	a centralized processing system that manages, or serves, files, data, and applications
Shared-service	the provision of a service by one part of the organization to other parts of the organization (like IT or HR services)
Silicon	semiconductor material for fabricating Integrated Circuit chips
System Admin	a person who is responsible for the upkeep, configuration, and reliable operation of the computer system
Tape (storage)	data storage medium using spools of magnetic tape which are played on tape drives
Telecom	abbreviation for Telecommunications
Time-to-market (TTM)	the length of time it takes from a product being conceived until its being available for sale
Tiered data storage	the assignment of different categories of data to various types of storage media to optimize the cost of storage
Virtual machine	an emulation of a computer system, i.e., a computer file, called an image, which behaves like an actual computer
Virtualization	the creation of a software-based, or virtual, representation of something (like a server), rather than a physical one
Voice-over-IP, VoIP	A technology for the delivery of voice and multimedia sessions over Internet Protocol (IP) networks, such as the Internet
Web 2.0	the next version of the World Wide Web, which emphasizes user-generated content and collaboration
Web browser	a software application for retrieving, presenting, and traversing information resources on the World Wide Web
Web services	software that makes itself available over the Internet as a service, and uses a standardized messaging system
Webserver	Computers that deliver (serve up) web pages. Every web server has an IP address and a domain name
World Wide Web	the combination of all resources and users on the Internet that are using the Hypertext Transfer Protocol (HTTP)
Y2K	an anticipated computer glitch related to date change from 1999 to 2000

Reviews

(Ashish Pachory's book on Business–Technology alignment) is a practical and useful guide to harnessing the power of Business–Technology alignment, which is an indispensable organizational requirement in this digital era. The book introduces the seven dimensions of alignment—culture, strategy, structure, process, intellect (innovation), function, and tactics—and explores their relevance as the building blocks of personal and enterprise success in the new era. Interspersed with simple and relatable examples, anecdotes, illustrations, tools, and exercises, the book is both interesting and pragmatic, having relevance for students and practitioners from all disciplines.

Dr. Bimal K. Malaviya
[Ph. D. Harvard University (Massachusetts Institute of Technology)]. Professor, Aerospace and Nuclear Engineering at Rensselaer Polytechnic Institute, Troy, New York.

(Ashish Pachory's book on Business–Technology alignment) is a book with a difference. It is a story of experiences skilfully woven to take you on a journey that would remind of several workplace challenges you dealt with while managing business affairs. Technology is all around and defines our way of life today. Business has become e-business and society has become e-society. We now talk about 5-10G, IoT, and Industry 4.0. These are terms beyond sense of integration. It refers to technology entrenched beyond any chance of visualizing it as separate entity. With business outcomes being increasingly influenced by information technology (IT), the alignment between Business and IT has become a crucial success factor for an enterprise in this digital age. This book is an intuitive and practical guide to discovering the power of Business–IT alignment and channeling it for personal and organizational growth. The many examples, exercises, and assessment tools in the book make it not only an insightful reference, but also a practical

handbook for managing real-world issues. It is an important read for practitioners and students alike.

Dr. M.P. Gupta
Head, Department of Management Studies, Indian Institute of Technology, Delhi

(Ashish Pachory's book on Business–Technology alignment) is an essential read for everyone who is, or aspires to be, in an organization that relies on technology to meet its business mission. An extract of years of experience with tips, tricks, and practical approaches not found in conventional textbooks and classrooms, it combines the need for Business–IT alignment with the strategic imperatives facing digital enterprises. Business–IT alignment is an indispensable organizational requirement in the digital era. Read this book to make it work for you as a real business enabler.

Wg Cdr A.B. Sharma
Founder and MD, Beyond Evolution Tech Solutions (P) Ltd., Member International Advisory Group (EU) on Trustworthy ICT, Formerly Managing Director at Globacom, Nigeria.

In a world where the very survival of business is dependent on the absorption, assimilation, and effective utilization of digital technology, business and technology are fast becoming indistinguishable from one another. The practical wisdom of this book will help organizations and individuals excel in this new world.

Amarendra Narayan
Former Secretary General, Asia Pacific Telecommunity (APT), Bangkok

It has indeed been a rewarding experience to have read this book. It very immaculately reintroduces us to concepts that we have always been aware of, but usually set aside for consideration later, in the prioritization between "the urgent and important." It is a book that makes one pause and wonder how so much got left to chance! It brings out very articulately the fact that, integrating technology with business is the basic mantra toward building profitable, sustainable, and long-lasting corporations.

Manoj Verma
Advisor and Consulting Partner (FMCG - Electrical), Ex CEO, Orient Electric, Ex-President, Consumer Business Unit, Crompton Greaves Ltd, Ex-President (ELCOMA – Apex Lighting Industry Association), Ex-Chairman (IFMA – Indian Fan Manufacturer`s Association)

The book covers a vital subject without burdening the reader with the complexities of business or the intricacies of technology. The basic concepts talked about in this book remind us of the need to seamlessly intertwine new technology with business basics.

Ashim Berry
Founder/CEO, KMS, Singapore, Leading Business Intelligence and Analytics solution provider in Asia Pacific.

References

1. Covey, S.R. 1989. *The Seven Habits of Highly Effective People*. FreePress.
2. Robert, S.K., and Norton, D.P. 1996. *The Balanced Score Card*. Harvard Business Review Press.
3. Pachory, A. 2019. *Aligning Technology with Business for Digital Transformation*. New York, NY: Business Express Press/Momentum Press.
4. Collins, J. 2001. *Good to Great*. HarperCollins.
5. About FedEx. 2018. Time Flies: FedEx Timeline https://about.van.fedex.com
6. de Bono, E. 2017. *The Six Thinking Hats*. London, UK: Penguin Books Ltd.
7. de Bono, E. 2016. *Lateral Thinking*. London, UK: Penguin Books Ltd.
8. There are several sources on the web for "7 leadership qualities of Eagles." No clear originator could be attributed. Examples: Carla Ibanzo, *7 powerful life lessons from the eagle,* (https://medium.com, Dec 2016) Jekyl, *Seven Leadership Qualities Derived From an Eagle*, (https://steemit.com/leadership, 2017).
9. Buzan, T. 2018. *Mind Map Mastery*. Watkins.
10. Gartner. 2019. Redefine IT's Business Value, https://gartner.com/en/information-technology/insights/business value-of-it,
11. DynamicCIO Achievers Series. 2013. The Innovative Heroes—Measuring IT's Impact on Business, 86. Grey Head Media.
12. Kotler, P. 1998. Marketing Management. Prentice-Hall Publications.
13. Ashish Pachory. 2014. ETCIO Q&A Session, cio.economictimes.indiatimes.com/cio-wall/ashish-pachory

About the Author

Ashish Pachory is an Information and Communication Technology (ICT) consultant and leadership guide. He was the Chief Information Officer (CIO) of the telecom services venture of the Tata group in India before venturing on his own. Before joining Tata in 2011, Ashish worked on the other side of the IT/Telecom value chain, in business, operations and delivery management functions with globally renowned companies like Nokia, Amdocs, Flextronics, Lucent (Bell-Labs), Hughes, and Wipro.

Ashish's work on measuring the business value of IT was recognized among the top IT innovations in 2013 by DynamicCIO (Achievers series). He was conferred Telecom Icon 2013 by Center of Recognition and Excellence (CORE) and recognized as one of India's most influential technology leaders (*Economic Times*). Also, in 2015, he was recognized among the top 25 global business CIOs by iCMG.

As a thought leader on technology trends and their adoption for business, he has been active as a speaker and panelist at industry forums and has contributed several thought-provoking articles and interviews in various industry and general publications, including the *Economic Times, The Business Standard, Information Week, Voice and Data*, and *CIO.com*.

Ashish is a telecommunications engineer and lives in Gurgaon (INDIA) with his wife, Seema. His interests include astronomy, reading, cryptic crosswords, and cricket.

He invites you to connect on LinkedIn or Twitter (@apachory) to share views and ideas.

Index

OTHER TITLES IN THE INFORMATION SYSTEMS COLLECTION

Daniel Power, University of Northern Iowa, Editor

- *Building Successful Information Systems* by Michael Savoie
- *Decision Support, Analytics, and Business Intelligence, Third Edition* by Daniel J. Power and Ciara Heavin
- *Successful ERP Systems* by Jack G Nestell and David L Olson
- *Computer Support for Successful Project Management* by Ulhas Samant
- *Data-Based Decision Making and Digital Transformation* by Daniel J. Power and Ciara Heavin

Announcing the Business Expert Press Digital Library

Concise e-books business students need for classroom and research

This book can also be purchased in an e-book collection by your library as

- a one-time purchase,
- that is owned forever,
- allows for simultaneous readers,
- has no restrictions on printing, and
- can be downloaded as PDFs from within the library community.

Our digital library collections are a great solution to beat the rising cost of textbooks. E-books can be loaded into their course management systems or onto students' e-book readers.
The **Business Expert Press** digital libraries are very affordable, with no obligation to buy in future years. For more information, please visit **www.businessexpertpress.com/librarians**. To set up a trial in the United States, please email **sales@businessexpertpress.com**.

www.ingramcontent.com/pod-product-compliance
Lightning Source LLC
Chambersburg PA
CBHW061215220326
41599CB00025B/4648